Seek Something Better

By Parker Bono

I dedicate this book to the American people and those who fight and fought for my right create this.

contents

Section 1 (Federal)

Section 2 (California)

Chapter 1
Views

"If you put the federal government in charge of the Sahara Desert, in five years there'd be a shortage of sand." -Milton Friedman

---

The below statements are my personal views on an array of subjects at the federal level.

Immigration

- A virtual wall will be built consisting of drones, surveillance, and other barriers that will end the potential for illegal immigration and plans that will end the incentive of it.

- Illegals currently in country will have the opportunity of work visas and at most permanent residence but never citizenship. If people with Visas or permanent residence have police confrontations (that aren't minor) then they will have to leave (deported).
- Immigrants must learn English (fed. Gov. will pay)
- Children of illegal immigrants should not receive citizenship even if they were born here. (from here on out)
- Hire 10,000 more border patrol agents.
- Eliminate sanctuary cities. Laws on immigration to the U.S. should be obeyed throughout the U.S. with no exceptions.

Guns

- The Second Amendment is a right but the amount of bullets those guns could hold isn't. We should be allowed to own guns with a background check and a maximum bullet capacity per magazine should hold a maximum amount of 16 bullets and there should be further screenings for people who attempt to buy guns. People who attempt to buy a gun should have to take a mandatory psychological test.

- The reason: 100 round clips are useless. This "Magazine Law" should be a national law as should further background checks/screenings/tests. Also, all instances of mass shootings are the result of crazy evil people with guns and a plethora of bullets.
- Eliminate "Gun Free Zones" in all of America.
- Allow concealed carry nationwide.

Foreign Policy

- Our military needs to be funded more. We have more growing threats from abroad and we need a strong military and that is something we currently lack.
- China and Russia have us beat right now both economically and militarily and we need more advanced technology rather than the same ideas. Our enemies become stronger and we become weaker.
- Foreign Terrorists should have no Constitutional rights.
- End the draft. If the war is worth fighting, people will volunteer.

- Continue to support our key ally Israel.
- Remain in NATO just make sure the other countries pay their fair share as we do.
  - Implementation of the URC
  - Attempt to make peace with North Korea.
- The U.S. should formally declare war on ISIS.
- Everything going on in the Middle East is because of a lack of power. You can overthrow a dictator but it's not going to solve anything. We must first take away all power then redistribute it in a democratic way to help form and maintain democracy in Middle Eastern countries that need it the most.
- Take out 50% of our troops located outside of the country.
- Create many more military aircrafts, boats, and submarines.
- Don't allow syrian refugees. (If there are 100 cookies and two are poisoned, do you eat one?)

Education

- We need to eliminate common core.

- Eliminate "Gun Free Zones" in schools (and have at least one armed official at each school)

Electoral

- ID required to vote to eliminate the possibility of voter fraud.
- Make election day a national holiday to ensure people have the time and opportunity to determine the future of their country.
- Make Election Day a National Holiday so it can be recognized for what it truly is, the most patriotic day of the year.
- Automatically register people to vote when you renew your driver's license.
- Campaign Finance Reform is wrong... "But to what extent can money buy power? Dismantling campaign finance laws can create more incentive for candidates to bend their will to the people who write the biggest checks. Yet money on its own clearly isn't enough to win a presidential race. Jeb Bush's super PAC raised more money in the first half of 2015 than President Obama's main super PAC did for the entire 2012 election cycle." -Forbes

Social

- Abortion should be illegal after 3 months.
- Continue to fund all aspects of Planned Parenthood other than abortion.
- Woman should make the same amount of money as a man if they have the same education or skill or experience as the man and companies should hire people as individuals.
- Government will support same sex marriage.
- Make smoking tobacco illegal since your stupidity shouldn't negatively affect someone else who didn't decide to smoke... AKA second hand smoke which kill over 55,000 each year, consisting mostly of children.

Environmental

- Global warming will continue to have many different views as to why it exists but it does exist. For this reason we as a country will try to "go green" not just for global warming but for health concerns.
- Expand offshore oil drilling
- GMO products should be labeled as GMOs as should Organic products.
- Wind energy can still be used but we should no longer offer tax credits for it.

We should also expand use of more efficient energy and use science to innovate currently existing technologies.

Economic

- Federal minimum wage should be raised from $7.25 to $10.00 gradually
- Physically and mentally capable people on welfare need to get a job and we need to help them get a job. (economical growth and unemployment rate will fall)
- Create more labor unions as they help the economy and are an efficient way for many to receive a job without needing special skills.
  - Flat income tax of 20%
  - Corporate income tax of 20%
- Social Security will be slowly eliminated. All people dependent on it, AKA who put money in will be given their current benefits and all people who haven't put money in won't need to but will need to put at least 3.5% of their income into a retirement fund that is not Government run. Our goal will be to write laws on what you do to retire rather than forcing you to put money into Social Security your whole life. This system will allow

businesses to compete for you and give Americans their own options for retirement and insure all people have enough money to have a good retirement and give individuals more money each year which will essentially help our economy.

- Create a maximum amount of time people can stay on welfare(1 year) so they have an incentive to get a job.
- People who deny a job should not receive welfare.

Domestic Policy

- Marijuana should be legalized but we need to crack down on the more deadly drugs, just take a different approach than the past failed war on drugs.
- There should be a term limit of 6 years for members of the House.
- People on "no-fly list" shouldn't be able to purchase a gun or ammunition.

Healthcare

- In order to attend public schools, students must receive certain vaccines.
- Some aspects of the Affordable care act need to be repealed while others need to be replaced. The middle class is

paying money they can't afford and receiving nothing in return.

- Healthcare should go beyond just a state level and all healthcare companies should compete nationwide.
- We should stop offering all forms of subsidization for illegal immigrants.

Criminal

- Police officers must wear body cameras. This protects the officer and the victim since there is a definitive answer to all the questions we may have.
- Convicted felons who did their time should have the right to vote.
- Solitary confinement should be banned for people under the age of 16.

Science

- The United States must return to space and manned space travel missions should be government funded.
- Study space to develop technologies revolved around it.
- Increase fundings for science and therefore innovation.

Chapter 2
Economics

"In economics, the majority is always wrong."
-John Galbraith

Since 1913, the year the Federal reserve was founded, the value of our currency has gone down over 90%. The Federal Reserve is the reason for our national debt. The Federal Reserve also benefits international bankers. The Federal Reserve will be eliminated and replaced with something else detailed in this plan.

They say that money doesn't grow on trees but actually, our current banking system creates currency faster than trees can grow. Also, our money is made of paper so it technically does. Most people don't understand our economy, yet alone how our currency is made/created, so i'll simplify it for you.

The system starts when political candidates say "Vote for me and i'll give you more stuff than my opponent will." But we know that nothing is life is free so this money has to come from somewhere. To fulfil their promise, the politicians spend more money than is available, and this is called deficit spending. To pay for this deficit spending, the U.S. Treasury borrows currency by issuing a bond. A bond, in case you didn't know, is basically an IOU. It's a piece of paper that promises to pay back the money you put in plus interest. What many don't know is that these bonds are our national debt. These bonds are to be payed back by the next generation.

Therefore, when the government issues a bond, it is taking prosperity out of the future for a quick cash flow it can have today. The treasury then holds a bond auction where the world bank's show up to buy part of our national debt in the form of bonds, and then they get to make a profit off of it in the form of interest. The international banks always benefit from our system and that will stop. I will explain how it will stop after I am done explaining the process.

Then, through open market operations, the banks sell the bonds to the Federal Reserve for a profit. To pay for these bonds, the Federal Reserve uses their checkbook and writes checks from an account with a $0 balance on it. Now, if you or I did this, it would be called fraud, but I guess it's totally fine for the Federal Reserve to do it. To quote the Boston Federal Reserve: "When you or I write a check, there must be sufficient funds in our account to cover the check, but when the Federal Reserve writes a check there is no bank deposit on which that check is drawn. When the Federal Reserve writes a check, it is creating money." A check is also an IOU. A check basically says "Here is an IOU for this much cash, now all you have to do is go to the bank and pick it up." After the Federal Reserve gives their checks to the bank, currency springs into existence. The banks then take that currency and buy more bonds from the U.S. Treasury. It's very important that you understand this whole process as it is key to understanding how it affects you and I.

To recap, the U.S. Treasury issues bonds, the banks buy those bonds with currency, the Federal Reserve write checks to the banks in exchange for the bonds, and currency is created. What's basically happening is that the Federal Reserve and the U.S. Treasury are just swapping checks and bonds, using the banks as middlemen, and evidently creating currency. This process continuously repeats, enriching the banks but indebting the public by rising the national debt. The final result is an excess of bonds at the Federal Reserve, and an excess of currency at the U.S. Treasury.

The next part of the system is when the U.S. Treasury deposits the new currency into different parts of the Government. The Government then does deficit spending by spending the money on public works, social programs, the military, etc. The Government employees then deposit their pay into the banks. This may be shocking but when you deposit your currency into the bank, you aren't actually depositing it into an account to be safely held or saved. Instead, you are loaning the bank your currency, and within legal limits, they can do with it basically whatever they want.

This is where the system gets crazy. This is where something called Fractional Reserve

Lending comes into play. Fractional Reserve Lending is the fact that Banks are allowed to reserve (or save) only a fraction of your deposit, and loan the rest out. Rates vary but for simplicity, I will use a 10% rate. If you make a $100 deposit into your account, in this scenario, the bank could take $90 of it and loan it out without letting you know. The bank must hold the $10 (10%) that you deposited, in case you want some. The $10 that actually got deposited is called vault cash. You may ask why your receipt says you have a $100 balance if the bank stole $90 of it and the answer is because the bank left an IOU called bank credit there in it's place. This may sound crazy, so here is a direct quote from the Federal Reserve Bank of New York, "Commercial banks create checkbook money whenever they grant a loan, simply by adding new deposit dollars in accounts on their books in exchange for a borrower's IOU" These are nothing but numbers typed into the bank's computers. And even though these numbers are very different from actual cash or currency since they only exist on a computer, they are still currency. So now, from your $100 deposit, there is now $190 in existence. Now, the only reason people take back loans from the banks is when they are going to buy something. So, the $90 that got loaned out will get spent by the borrower on something and the money will go to the seller. But then the seller deposits money into his bank account, and his bank loans out 90% of that, or $81 out to someone else, and leaves bank credit numbers in it's place. SO now there is $271 in existence. This process continuously repeats until a deposit of just $100 can create up to $1,000 in bank credit, all backed by $100 in vault cash, or just 10%. In other words, your $100 deposit sprung $900 into existence. But as I said, ratios vary from 0% to 10% to 20%, and so on. The result is that the currency expansion is far greater than even this example makes you believe.

To recap, when currency is deposited into the banks, the banks can lend it out, and then it gets re-deposited and relent over and over again creating bank credit each time. This is where the majority of our currency supply comes from. In fact, it is estimated that 92%-96% of all currency in the U.S. is created not by the Government but by the banking system.

Lots of currency getting put into society may sound like a good idea at first until you realize that the prices of everyday goods and services act as a sponge on an expanding currency supply. The more currency that we have, the more things will cost. This is called inflation. The definition of inflation is an expansion of the currency supply. Rising prices are simply a symptom of inflation. So basically our entire currency supply is nothing but a couple of bucks put into the scam where the Federal Reserve and the U.S. Treasury swap IOUs and a bunch of numbers banks type into their computers. And as crazy as that sounded, this part is even crazier. We the people work for a portion of that currency supply. True wealth is your time but we trade away tens of thousands of hours for numbers that somebody printed on pieces of paper or typed into their computer. Now these numbers represent our blood sweat and tears. We the people are what give the currency its value. But here comes the craziest part. We work hard so we can save some of that currency so we can pay the tax collectors or the IRS. The IRS then gives that money to the U.S. Treasury so that way they can pay the principal plus interest on the bond that the Federal Reserve bought with a check drawn on an account with a balance of $0. Yes that;s right, much of our taxes don't go to schools or public services but to pay interest on the bonds that the Federal Reserve bought with a check drawn from an account that has nothing in it. As i stated previously, the Federal Reserve is committing fraud. But here is a very unknown secret. Before the implementation of the Federal Reserve in 1913, there was no need for a personal income tax. In 1913, the Federal Reserve was founded. That same year, the Constitution was amended to allow income tax. Do you really think that this was a coincidence? Just think of how much income tax you have payed in your lifetime. Then think of the amount of that that was silently transferred into the hands of those who own the system. Yes, this system has owners, and who they are is an even bigger secret I will address next.

But first, you need to understand the lie of the debt ceiling. The debt ceiling is based on a paradox. There was interest due on that bond, and there was interest due on every one of those loans that the banks made. This means that there is interest due on every single dollar that is in existence. Let me ask you something:

If you borrow the very first dollar into existence, and that's the only dollar that exists in the U.S., but you promise to pay it back plus another dollar worth of existence, where do you get the other dollar from? The answer is you have to borrow that one into existence and promise to pay it back as well. So now there are two dollars in existence but you owe 4 dollars. (This process continues indefinitely and the result is there is never enough currency left to pay off the debt. This of course is excluding the assets the U.S. owns that are key in my plan to end the National Debt that will be achieved over an 8 year period) Therefore, the whole system is impossible.It is finite and it will come to an end one day even if we never got rid of the Federal Reserve.

The founding fathers of the United States knew about the dangers of central banking and fought to free themselves from this very thing. The Revolutionary War started off as a tax revolt. But now we must pay tax just to have a monetary system. After they suffered from the hyperinflation of the Continental Dollar that was printed in excess just fund the Revolutionary War, they understood the dangers of fiat currency. So to protect future generations from theft and out of control government, they wrote into the Constitution that "{No State shall} make any Thing but gold and silver Coin a Tender in Payment of Debts." They did this for the simple fact that you can't print gold and silver. Our current system isn't just unconstitutional but also robs us of what our founding fathers fought and died for. We all feel the effects of neglecting the Constitution right now. By forcing more currency into circulation, our purchasing power plummets. Inflation is a slow tax that is simply the result of this monetary system.

This system benefits those who create the currency and receive it first as they get to spend it into circulation before it has an effect on the economy. They are stealing purchasing power from you and giving it to the banks and the government every day. It's not like the people at the top don't know this. To quote the Federal Reserve, "The decrease in purchasing power incurred by holders of money due to inflation imparts gains to the issuers of the money." This whole system is fraudulent. Our whole system is nothing but a system of legalized theft.

This is the biggest con of it all. The Federal Reserve is not entirely federal. It has stockholders. There is no federal agency that has stockholders. A share of stock represents a percentage of ownership in an organization. This means that those shareholders are the owners of this organization. This makes the Federal Reserve a private corporation with owners. We know that the Federal Reserve has stockholders because if you go the the Federal Reserve's website, you will see that it states the stockholders receive an annual dividend of 6 percent. We know that in the beginning, these shareholders were the largest banks in the United States but due to company mergers and acquisitions throughout the years, we don't actually know who these shareholders are. I would assume that the owners are the banks that make a profit by selling part of our national debt in the forms of bonds to Federal Reserve who buys them with a check from nothing.

This system funnels wealth from working Americans to the government and the banks. It is the pure cause of the artificial good times and bad times of modern economies. This system is also only possible because we use currency, not real money like gold and silver as the Constitution states we shall. But worst of all, it is a form of enslavement. Nobody asked you if you wanted to pay tax today for the prosperity that we enjoyed throughout the last century. To quote George Washington, "No generation has the right to contract debts greater than can be paid off during the course of their own existence." By stealing prosperity of tomorrow for purposes today, we enslave ourselves and future generations. This all sounds very bad but there is hope. You are the greatest threat to this system. If you load and cock the gun, I will aim and shoot it. When I am elected President, I will fix it. I will fix this system by...

- Achieving 0% Unemployment
- Auditing and ending the Federal Reserve
- Promoting small business
- Giving a 0.000002% Tax Deduction per employee a company hires.
- Infrastructure growth and development
- Forcing the unemployed to volunteer
- Reforming welfare and immigration
- Import Tax

- Offer 1% tax deductions for companies that make products in the U.S.A.
- Offer 1% tax deductions for companies that hire

Plan	How many jobs we have lost since 2008	How many jobs we would gain in 8 years
Lowering Corporate Income Tax	2,500,000	3,000,000
Tax credit for made in U.S.A. items	0	1,000,000
Offering tax credits for each worker a company hires	0	1,000,000
Promoting small businesses and	2,000,000	2,000,000

innovation		
Offering incentives for companies and workers who hire or are hired to ecommerce jobs	1,000,000	7,000,000
True Immigration Reform	16,000,000	7,000,000

Below is my tax plan.

Current Federal Tax Rate	Future Federal Tax Rate
10%-39.6%	20%

Future Corporate Tax Rate	Current Corporate Tax Rate	Corporation Annual Income
10%	15%-39%	Under $400,000
20%	35%-38%	Above $400,000

Total Non-Federal Tax Rate	Future State Tax Rates	Future Local Tax Rates	Current State Tax Rates	Current Local Tax Rates
No More Than 7.5%	No More Than 5%	No More Than 2.5%	0%-7.5%	0%-5%

No American Can Be Taxed More Than 27.5%!

(Including Federal, State, And Local Taxes)

This Tax Plan is the simplest our nation has ever seen and will give the American people, particularly the middle class, great amounts of tax cuts, and will therefore give our economy tremendous growth.

Below is the future federal budget I would enact as President

NAT SPENDING (WITH NAT DEBT INCLUDED)
SOURCES OF INCOME (Annually)...
Corporate Tax(20%)- 400 Billion
Income Tax(15% Flat Tax)- 2 Trillion
Payroll Taxes(Same rate)- 1 Trillion
Other Taxes- 300 Billion
TOTAL: 3.8 Trillion

SPENDING
Social Security, Unemployment, And Labor- 1.3 Trillion
Health- 1 Trillion
Military- 550 Billion
Veterans Affairs- 150 Billion
Interest- 250 Billion

Education, Training, Employment, And Social Services- 100 Billion
Science- 50 Billion
Transportation- 100 Billion
Other- 175 Billion
TOTAL: 3.65 Trillion
125 Billion Surplus Each Year (Excluding Debt Plan)
AFTER 8 YEARS: 1 Trillion

Below is my plan to end the National Debt. All sources of revenue under these bullet points will be directed towards the National Debt.
I will...

- Raise All Excise Taxes 20% (10% Goes To 12%) *75 Billion Annually*
- Eliminate Loopholes And Some Credits *225 Billion Annually*
- Increase Tax Rate For Medicare Hospital Insurance By 1% *100 Billion Annually*
- Raise Federal Cigarette Tax Rate By $5 Per Pack *50 Billion Annually*
- 20% Tax On All Imports *500 Billion Annually*
- End War On Drugs *25 Billion Annually*

- Drill For Oil In The Green River Formation (Extract 5% Of Total Oil There Annually) *2.5 Trillion Annually (In Profit)*
- Legalize And Tax Marijuana And Online Gambling *50 Billion Annually*

EACH YEAR= 2.5 Trillion off of debt (Includes surplus from budget)
AFTER 8 YEARS: Surplus/elimination of national debt

This is my plan to save the middle class.

The middle class is currently being destroyed. The upper class is paying small amounts of money that they can easily afford. The lower class is receiving money from both the middle and the upper class for basically doing nothing and the middle class is paying money they can't afford. Middle class American's don't have access to what upper or lower class americans have access to. This puts the middle class at a huge disadvantage. My plan would change that.

Goals of the Middle Class Plan:
- Raise wages and increase the annual income for middle class americans
  - Give the middle class more opportunities
- Don't make the middle class pay for things they can't afford
- Create more good jobs that pay well
- Eliminate wage theft that happens to 20% of men and 30% women.

How it will be achieved:
- Raising the minimum wage will definitely help middle class americans since they will be paid more as well. Also, by eliminating social security, Americans will make 6.5% more every year.
- One way to give the middle class more opportunities is to open up many corporate jobs that would pay well. Millions of these jobs will be available since many companies will be returning to the U.S.
- The middle class can no longer afford to pay as much as they do. This is why

there should be a flat income tax of 20%, with exceptions to the lower class. This would be fair to the middle class and allow them to earn more money each year. Also, if there was a maximum amount Americans could be taxed, that would help ensure that there is no chance that the middle class is taken advantage of yet again.

- If Americans wanted good paying jobs, the best solution would be unions. If Americans had the freedom to create and join unions as they wanted, well paying jobs would increase and the middle class would benefit.
- We should also eliminate wage theft. It happens far too often and it is wrong. It happens to 20% of men and 30% of women and it happens even more to people of color. If it was totally eliminated, everyone would receive more money.

Effects:
- Middle class Americans would make more money.
- Middle class Americans would receive better jobs.

- Middle class Americans would pay less in taxes each year.
- More unions would be created, so the economy would improve drastically.
- Wage theft would be eliminated so all Americans would no longer be wrongfully robbed of their well deserved money.
- The middle class would thrive once again, as it should!

Below will be the future trade policy in our nation.

Goals Of Trade Plan
- Bring China to the bargaining table
- Reclaim millions of American's jobs
- Strengthen our negotiation position
- Make companies come back to America.
- Make money rather than lose money every year on trade with China, as well as the rest of the world

How It Will Be Achieved:
- Declare China a currency manipulator.
- End China's Intellectual Property Violations which costs us $300 Billion and many jobs every year.
- Eliminate other countries unfair advantages.
- Tax countries 30% for all imported goods.

- Lower the corporate income tax to China's (30%) and make it a flat tax.
- Offer tax credits if you buy items or goods made in the U.S.
- End our National Debt and Deficit.

Effects:
- Companies would return to America
  - Tens of millions of jobs would be available, making the U.S. a target for immigration (that would be done legally), and giving hope once again to the American Dream.
- The U.S. would make money on trade each year rather than lose money.
- China would finally get what it deserves for being corrupt for the last 20 years.

This is my plan regarding jobs and job growth in our nation.

Supposedly, about 6% of Americans are unemployed. I don't necessarily believe this number but we can still use it even though many of those people who aren't considered unemployed solely gave up looking for a job or were offered one but declined or were laid off or possibly even getting their money from extreme forms of welfare. Regardless, that number should still be far under 6% and it will if we follow this plan as designed... We need Jobs, an increased GDP, and a booming economy and we need it now!

Goals of the Jobs Plan:
- To lower unemployment rate to less than 1% by the end of two terms
- Create over 20 Million jobs by the end of two terms
- Lower inflation rates
- Raise GDP (Gross Domestic Product) by 50% or more
- Raise net worth of family earnings by 30% or more
- Lower interest rates
- Bring U.S. markets to all time highs and prove to Americans it is beneficial to save and invest
- Lower taxes to compete/match China
- Bring companies to the U.S.

How this will happen:
- Flat Corporate Income Tax and Income Tax of 20% (with exceptions to very small or poor people). This system will be modeled after China and will allow us to compete with China. Also stop taxing capital gains.
- Create a "Reverse Inversion" (reversion is when companies leave the U.S.). With the 20% Corporate Income Tax.

- Our next goal will be to make companies bring their estimated $2 Trillion parked offshore back home as well. We will do this by just taxing that by 10% when they come back (one time). This would result in the government receiving $200 Billion in taxes and allow $1.8 Trillion to go into the economy.
- Thirdly, we are going to want to make sure people buy the products made in the U.S. We will do this by giving tax credits to people when they buy products that are U.S. made.
- After we secure the border, we will offer many temporary visas, or in many cases permanent residence but NEVER citizenship. They give up their right to vote when they come here illegally. Many people that come here demand a job and food stamps and when we give them that and they don't have to pay taxes, our economy falls.
- Increase reserve requirements on the amount of money banks are legally required to keep on hand to cover withdraws. The more money banks are required to hold back, the less they have

to lend to consumers. If they have less
to lend, consumers will borrow less,
which will decrease spending.

Chapter 3
Security

"There are some who've forgotten why we have a military. It's not to promote war, it's to be prepared for peace" -Ronald Reagan

---

These are my goals regarding foreign policy.

As our relations with other countries changes drastically, Foreign Policy is a key factor to look at. We must find a way to be the greatest country in the world and have the greatest military in the world and ensure safety to our homeland and our allies. We must also ensure that countries like China pay their fair share. Some of our current enemies should also begin to become neutral or friendly, if possible-otherwise impose so many sanctions that the country is forced to comply. We can prosper, be the best, and we can create peace and we will under this plan!

Goals of the Foreign Policy Plan:
- To create peace
- To show power
- To protect in exchange for protection

- To defeat ISIS
- Stop patrolling the world
- Ensure that admission into the greatest country is exclusive to the greatest people who would like to immigrate here.

How it will happen:

- Negotiate and speak with other countries and prove it's beneficial to be allies or neutral rather than enemies.
- Fund our military more.
- Make members of NATO pay their fair share.
- Do many more airstrikes and put a small amount of highly skilled members of the military to defeat ISIS and have them come out every 6 months and send a new group of 250 in.
- Take back half of military members stationed outside of the U.S.
- Create a queue that applies when trying to immigrate to the U.S.

Effects:

- Relations with countries would improve.
- Our military will be the strongest in the world.

- We will be the most powerful country in the world.
- NATO members would do as they should.
- ISIS as we know it would be eliminated within 4 years.
- We would have half as many troops deployed overseas.
- A queue system would be applied to the immigration process.

This is a plan to ensure safety is given to all Americans.

Safety should be insured to all americans, no matter the location or ethnicity or place or time. This however is something that we currently lack as many Americans don't feel safe, many Americans are not safe, and many children are forced to grow up feeling just as scared as things as their parents are. Under my plan, every American would be able to feel safe in their own homes or at any public place.

Goals of the Safety Plan:
- To ensure safety is provided to all Americans
- To bring terrorism to an all time low
- To bring death to an all time low

- To ensure relations between Americans is at an all time high.
- To ensure all Americans are safe and feel safe.

How it will happen:
- People who could possess a threat will be punished and caught. We will make sure people are willing to speak up. People will start talking and stop doing terrible crimes.
- We will create a more sophisticated background check system. This would allow the good to come and the bad to leave. We will also survey areas all across america to ensure there are no chances of anything occurring. We will also have one armed person at every public place. These guns will always be supplied by the government and in some instances, the people with them will be supplied by the government as well.
- Death, that is typically gang related, will be dealt with. We will break up gangs.
- Many americans don't trust each other, for obvious- but wrong reasons. This would stop as we would prove that it is

safe and beneficial to be friendly and trust each other.
- Many Americans don't feel safe. For all the reasons listed above and many more, they will begin to feel safe again and they will be kept safe.

Effects:
- Americans would be guaranteed safety.
  - Terrorism in the U.S. would fall.
  - Death- typically gang related- will be dealt with, as will gangs in general.
  - Relations among Americans would reach an all time high.
- Safety will be restored to all Americans.

Chapter 4
Health

"If you like your doctor or healthcare plan, you can keep it." -Barack Obama

This quote was a blatant lie as premiums rose on average over 50%, thousands of doctors quit, many people had to change their plans and go to the Obamacare Bronze plan where you can't even get a percocet, and the middle class was once again penalized for trying to live. Below is my healthcare plan.

Welfare recipients should receive a form of healthcare that in case of an emergency, will cover them. This however would only last one year (6 months while they search for a job and 6 months while they earn money from a job.)

My healthcare plan would...
1. Repeal some parts of Obamacare and rewrite some other parts.
2. Remove the individual mandate.
3. Break away state barriers on health care providers.
4. Make health care savings accounts tax free and encourage use of them.
5. Make Medicaid a state level issue, not a Federal.Cut federal funding in half.
6. Allow oversea drug imports. This will drastically decrease prices.

Below is my plan for the future of Social Security.

Social Security, the term used to described a flawed system that has been stealing from Americans for generations. All Social Security is is an inter-generational transfer of wealth-and this transfer effects the next generation more and more every time. It's time to end the flawed system that gives out more money than it can afford to give and give Americans and other companies more opportunities. Americans will get what they deserve in my plan!

Basically, we are going to end social security and write new laws about retirement funds. Kind of like the Affordable Care Act, we won't present another government run retirement program rather laws for currently existing and future ones.

Firstly, eliminating Social Security would give Americans about 6.5% more of their income each year. Then, our new laws will require Americans to put a minimum of 3.5% of their income into a retirement fund. Assuming you make the current average salary in America ($55,775) and invest the minimum (3.5%) into a retirement account, you would have about $600,000 in savings when you retire (at age 67) and if you live to the average life expectancy (age 79) then you would collect about $50,000 each year in pensions during your retirement or $4,150 a month. This assumes the average inflation rate of 3%. Instead, if you made that same annual income each year, and paid it into Social Security, your monthly pension payment would be about $2,500. This also equates in 3% annual inflation. The new law would provide the average American with $2,000 more each month as opposed to Social Security pensions with the same annual income, starting age, retirement age, and inflation rate yet you are taxed 3% more... and the government still finds a way to spend more than they have on this program.

The problem is this can't all happen over night. If it did, very bad things would happen although it would be beneficial in the long run. Instead, we will take everyone who hasn't put money into Social Security off of it as well as people born in the future. The situation for the already retried and people who have already put money in will remain the same until they die. Future adult workers will have to pay at least 3.5% of their income into a retirement savings account and future generations will have a much more prosperous retirement.

Chapter 5
Domestic Plans

"The Constitution only guarantees the American people the right to pursue happiness. You have to catch it yourself." -Benjamin Franklin

---

This is my plan regarding the reformation of the welfare system.

About 1 out of every 3 Americans are on some form of welfare. Many of these Americans may need help, but what we are offering isn't efficient. We give enough money out each year in welfare programs to bring each person on welfare 4 times above the poverty line but because of misuse of the funds, many programs are wasteful. It's time for Reformation! Also, many people are dependent on free stuff welfare offers rather than going out and doing something. The current welfare system encourages dependence and costs the middle class far too much!

"Taxpayers today are paying the poorest people in America a trillion dollars a year not to work. And so that is what they are doing in response. In 1960, nearly two-thirds of U.S. households in the lowest-income one-fifth of the population were headed by persons who worked. But after the War on Poverty began in 1965, by 1991 this work effort had declined by about 50 percent, with only one-third of household heads in the bottom 20 percent in income working at all, and only 11 percent working full-time, year-round. One central reason for the inequality between the top 20% and the bottom 20% is that according to the Census Bureau families in the top 20% work 16

times as much as families in the bottom 20%."
-Forbes.com- 2016.

I will...
- CAP WELFARE SPENDING AT $200 BILLION ((FEDERAL))
- ($250 BILLION SAVED EACH YEAR)
- MAKE ALL FORMS OF WELFARE HAVE A ONE YEAR MAXIMUM
- ELIMINATE CORPORATE WELFARE!

These plans will save each taxpayer about $1,500.

Welfare plans that will be eliminated (with current cost per year)
1. Lifeline, AKA Obamaphone-3B
2. LIHEAP-5B
3. WIC-10B

Many others that would add up to about another 38B.

Welfare plans we will lower spendings for (with current cost per year)
1. Child Nutrition- From 25B to 20B
2. EITC- From 85B to 75B
3. SNAP- From 80B to 50B
4. HUD- From 50B to 40B
5. SSI- From 56B to 30B
6. Medicaid- From 500B to 400B

Many others that will be addressed in per category plan...

Welfare plans we will expand (with future and current cost per year)

1. Pell Grants- From 35B to 50B
2. TANF- From 16B to 50B
3. Head Start- From 10B to 20B
4. Job Training- From 6B to 50B

If we do this and the other things that are addressed in the per category plan, our future will have many opportunities to do much better than we currently are doing.

Below is my per sector welfare plan regarding funding.

Category	Current Spending (In Billions)	Future Spending (In Billions)	Total Change (In Billions)
Cash	200	125	-75
Medical	600	500	-100
Food	100	75	-25

Housing	50	75	+25
Energy	5	5	0
Education	40	75	+35
Training	10	50	+40
Services	15	15	0
Child Care	20	30	+10
Community Development	10	15	+5
Other	100	25	-75

We will also make all welfare Insurance recipients as well as welfare payment recipients who are unemployed volunteer until they find a job and they can only stay on welfare for one year. This way they earn job experience and contribute to the economy so in a way, they are earning the money.

Final: Save 200 Billion each year from taxpayers that pay into welfare and expand forms of welfare that have the greatest chances of creating success for families and individuals in the future.

"PEOPLE ON WELFARE WILL BE ENCOURAGED TO WORK, TRAINED TO WORK, AND THEY WILL WORK. CHILDREN WILL BE TREATED WITH IMMENSE RESPECT AND WILL HAVE A GREAT OPPORTUNITY TO BE A PART OF GREATNESS THAT RESIDES WITHIN OUR GREAT COUNTRY AND THE AMERICAN DREAM! ALSO, OUR MIDDLE CLASS AMERICANS WILL NO LONGER SUFFER TO PAY FOR SOMEONE ELSE TO SUFFER EVEN MORE WHILE ON WELFARE!"

Below are future policies regarding immigration.

Every year, millions of people from all over the world, but mainly Mexico, immigrate to the United States of America illegally. The result is the fact that many American's jobs are being taken away, drugs and crime coming through to the U.S. at rate that is definitely noticeable, and people who don't pay taxes yet still receive tens of billions of dollars in free education benefits, free healthcare benefits, free housing benefits, and free food stamp benefits, which costs Americans even more money. These results are not beneficial to America and therefore illegal immigration needs to come to an end and legal immigration needs to come to a new high. Immigrants who pay taxes like every other American citizen do indeed help our economy so we should let them come in legally just make sure they would be great enough for the greatest country in the world. We would do this by hiring more workers and doing far more sophisticated background checks but making it so those background checks are done quicker so people aren't stuck on the waiting list for years.

The current immigration system allows the following to happen: drugs to pour through, illegal immigrants to be housed in our prisons, a violent drug war to exist, gang violence to be brought to the U.S., and loss of jobs that could be given to unemployed Americans. All of these catastrophes can be prevented if we follow all of the ideas listed below. We will give higher rankings in the queue for immigrants who pass the background check and can prove they are able to do skill required jobs. This would make the unemployment rate fall, allow them to make money, and allow the government to make more money! This queue system would also help our economy. We should also defund sanctuary cities. U.S. immigration laws should be followed throughout the U.S. without exceptions. We should also increase punishments for overstaying a Visa. We should deport all criminal aliens currently in our prisons being funded by our taxpayers. We will give out permanent residency and visas to certain families and deport others, depending on the situation. We need to build a virtual wall since that is the most efficient method. This virtual wall would consist of sophisticated monitorization technology, including drones. We also will hire more border patrol agents, which will create jobs, and monitor more heavily other ways illegal immigrants come into our country such as through planes. Many other countries have walls to help stop illegal immigration from occurring. This number actually adds up to 35% of the countries in the world (65 to be exact) that have border walls, and the U.S. would be the 66th. We should also create a nationwide e-verify system, which would protect jobs for all unemployed americans. Finally, we should end birthright citizenship which is the largest magnet for illegal immigration. You should not be granted citizenship for being the child of an illegal immigrant, even if you were born here. That may sound wrong but it really isn't. In 85% of the world, birthright citizenship is illegal. If we do this, our country and it's economy would improve drastically!

This is a plan regarding the future of the FDA.

People are going to question why I am going after the FDA and to that I will question why the FDA is going after us by allowing dangerous ingredients to be put in our foods, being a very corrupt administration, and regulating over 20% of our economy. The FDA typically has a straightforward answer to drugs: make sure it is safe and effective if it is to be legal. It is essential that we continue to have monitorization of foods and chemicals and conduct studies that show side effects. This however isn't done well with the FDA. This, along with many other reasons, is why we must reform the FDa... and here's how to do it.

The process for approving new drugs in the U.S. takes a long time and costs a lot of money. But in trying to speed things up too much, Congress runs the risk of allowing drugs to reach the market that aren't necessarily safe. This will no longer be allowed. The FDA will not allow the use of any food or drug that has not passed their studies. We also will immediately recall an item if it begins to go under FDA investigation.

We all want our products to be safe but the FDA spends so much time trying to prove products are clinically useful which should be the job of patients and doctors. We will make it faster for drug companies to get approval by cutting the target review time of 10 months to five months which would also make drugs less expensive. Now Grandma and Grandpa don't need to spend over 10% of their Social Security check on drugs. Also, more breakthroughs would be made and more options would be available because more companies would enter the drug market.

We will immediately stop the fluoridation of water and will conduct a non biased FDA study on it for the first time in U.S. history. Over 23 human studies and over 100 animal studies linked fluoride to brain damage. Fluoride is the only drug forced as mass medication of the population despite the fact that once fluoride is added to the water supply, there is no way of controlling the dose; it goes to everyone regardless of age, weight, health, need, or nutritional status. Tooth decay, AKA the only supposed reason we fluoridate our water, has been found to be going down at a faster rate in non fluoridated countries than fluoridated countries. It is estimated that 41% of U.S. children have some form of dental fluorosis caused by excess fluoride. Finally, only 1% of the fluoridated water is consumed by humans... 99% of the fluoridated water goes down the drain and into the environment. Assuming the FDA study on fluoride shows the same result as almost every study on fluoride, we will permanently stop poisoning our own citizens.

Drug prices are on an extreme rise. Most recently, EpiPen prices have been going up a very substantial amount. EpiPen could only raise prices because they had no competition in the marketplace. That's odd, given that epinephrine isn't patented and has been synthesized for well over a century. In Europe, there are multiple competitors to EpiPen, but in the United States, the FDA has prevented competitors from entering the market – and the biggest competitor to EpiPen, Adrenaclick, is barred from substitution for EpiPen in prescriptions. We will immediately allow free market competition for the EpiPen and will stop allowing lobbyists to control what is regulated or not by the FDA.

In the past, the FDA has done many horribly corrupt things. Just some consist of faked X-ray reports, forged retinal scans, phony lab tests, and secretly amputated limbs. These were all done by FDA scientists that figured they could get away with it. Most don't know about this because when the FDA finds scientific fraud or misconduct, the agency doesn't notify the public, the medical establishment, or even the scientific community that the results of a medical experiment are not to be trusted. On the contrary. For more than a decade, the FDA has shown a pattern of burying the details of misconduct. As a result, nobody ever finds out which data is bogus, which experiments are tainted, and which drugs might be on the market under false pretenses. The FDA has repeatedly hidden evidence of scientific fraud not just from the public, but also from its most trusted scientific advisers, even as they were deciding whether or not a new drug should be allowed on the market. We want the FDA to have much more freedom but only to an extent. We must simply implement policies that make sure this doesn't happen and punish the ones who did it if it is done.

The FDA has let some ingredients through that should have never been given to the public... You, your children, your parents, etc. My FDA commissioner will order the banning of the drugs listed below for reasons that are also listed below.

Ingredient	Reason It Should Be Banned

Olestra/Olean	blocks the body's ability to absorb essential minerals and vitamins.
Brominated Vegetable Oil (BVO)	Increases the risk of breast cancer, prostate cancer, ovary cancer, thyroid problems and cause death in children.
Potassium Bromate	linked to kidney problems, neurological disorder and cancer.
BHA/BHT	insomnia, increased appetite, loss of energy, liver and kidney damage, fetal abnormalities, mental and physical retardation, cancer and baldness.
Azodicarbonamide	asthma and allergies.
Artificial food coloring and synthetic food dyes	linked to neurological problems, brain cancer, ADD, ADHD and hyperactivity.

rBGH or rBST hormones	linked to breast and prostate cancer, thyroid disease, diabetes, obesity, infertility, asthma and allergies.
Neonicotinoid pesticides	linked to colony collapse of bees.
Arsenic	causes cancer or even death
Formaldehyde	can damage human cell and long term exposure to Formaldehyde can cause cancer including leukemia and short term exposure can cause watery or burning eyes, asthma, headaches, skin irritation, and nausea.
Potassium Bromate	causes cancer in the thyroids, kidneys and other body parts
GM Corn	severe stomach inflammation and enlargement of the

	uterus
GM Soybeans	allergies, sterility, and birth defects

Below is a my plan regarding the VA.

The current VA has allowed over 300,000 veterans to die waiting for care. This of course was wrongly excused. This must and will come to an end.

Goals of the Veterans Plan:
- Modernize the VA
- Insure that our veteran's invisible wounds are recognized and helped.
- Stop corruption and fraud that currently exists in the VA
- Ensure veterans have easy access to healthcare that would help them and their needs.

How it will be achieved:
- Fire the current VA executives.
- Increase funding for PTSD, traumatic brain injury, and suicide prevention so

our veteran's and their invisible wounds
are recognized.

- Create a plan that is affiliated with the VA that gives all veterans access to healthcare.
- Modernizing technology used in the VA.

Effects:

- Fraud would be eliminated from the VA after the firing of the current executives.
- The VA would be modernized. The Veterans Plan would make it happen by accelerating and expanding investments in state of the art technology to deliver best-in-class care quickly and effectively. All veterans should be able to conveniently schedule appointments, communicate with their doctors, and view accurate wait times with the push of a button.
- All veterans would have access to healthcare that is run by the VA.
- The injuries associated with veterans would be recognized, diagnosed, and solved. This would drastically improve the health of our veterans.

This is my plan regarding criminals and the law.

Every year the failed war on drugs causes many people to be charged for drug use more harshly than murderers are charged. Also, many past felons still don't have the right to vote. They are americans and their voice matters just as much as ours. The death penalty should remain for certain cases and we should crack down on the more dangerous drugs but legalize recreational use of marijuana.

Goals of the Criminal Plan:
- To ensure all Americans get to use their right to vote.
- To ensure equality in sentencing.
- To enforce strict punishments for strict laws that were broken.
- To reform the war on drugs and instead work on rehabilitation more than punishment.

How it will be achieved:
- Laws would be changed to give past felons the right to vote.
- Sentences would have new requirements so stricter law breakers receive stricter punishments and smaller law breakers receive more minor punishments.
- Offer rehabilitation to drug and alcohol abuser, etc.

LEGALIZE RECREATIONAL USE OF MARIJUANA
^GOOD SOURCE OF TAX REVENUE^

Effects:
- No voting rights will be falsely taken away.

- People will be fairly charged and fairly punished.
- Strict and minor lawbreakers will receive strict and minor punishments.
- Less criminals will commit second offenses.
- People will no longer import marijuana (The #1 drug that comes illegally to the U.S.) illegally since they can go anywhere else rather than buy it illegally.

Chapter 6
Miscellaneous

"One of the penalties for refusing to participate in politics, is that you end up being governed by your inferiors." -Plato

---

This is a brief statement on my current view of our nation as well as what we must do to fix it.

"Although America is brainwashed, the spirit of America will never die!" -Parker, 2016

Right now, our country is at a turning point. We are facing problems in many ways and we need someone who is willing to identify those problems and do something about them. Here at home, we feel as though people deserve equal result rather than equal opportunity. All people deserve the same opportunity to succeed but what you do with it is up to you.

Extreme forms of welfare ensures people are stuck and dependent on welfare since i keep getting a small amount of stuff for free so I don't go out and do anything. Economically, we need to replace NAFTA and bring jobs home. We lost over 1,000,000 jobs to NAFTA and have lost far more to China. We treat small businesses terribly and larger corporations even worse. If we lowered our corporate income tax, companies may actually want to come back. Right now, they have no incentive to stay! Our markets are fine but could and should be doing much better.

At the border, we are faced with a crisis. Illegal Immigrants are rewarded for coming here illegally, and the fact that they are even able to come here illegally in the first place says a lot. We could fix this by creating a virtual wall with drones, surveillance, and many other forms of innovative technology. Then there's the "Syrian Refugees". Here's a good analogy about them: Imagine there are 100 cookies but 2 are poisoned. Do you risk it and eat one? Roughly about 98% of the time, they are most likely good people but because of the fact we can't really vett them, all we can look at is the fact that there are some bad. Besides, they have many other places they can go and at this time we just can't afford to take any risks. I'd suggest us helping them go to another country but not admit any into our country. Saudi Arabia has over 100,000 tents with perfectly running water and electricity they can go to.

Guns have seemed to split America into a divisive two when there is a simple and logical answer to it all. Rather than ban a type of gun, how about we encourage gun ownership but at the same time enforce fool proof screenings/psychological tests. We can't just hand out guns and we shouldn't take away rights either. This way, America will be safer and both sides will be happier. We could also restrict the amount of bullets in guns as well to 16. This is solely to prevent the possible damage that could be done if our system fails and because 100 round clips are useless. We will also eliminate "Gun Free Zones" in all of America. This is because you don't need to write laws for good people and the bad people don't care about those laws. All these zones do is set up targets. We should eliminate gun free zones and have armed officials at all current gun free zones. This helps minimize or eliminate the damage potentially done.

One of the most detrimental programs called Social Security will be ended and replaced with laws about retirement. We simply can not continue Social Security as it is terrible on both sides. The government has to spend more on it rather than other programs that are far more beneficial and the people must pay more in taxes. It must change! Another detrimental policy called the Affordable Care Act will be repealed and replaced but not entirely. In the end, it will work out for everyone.

Here at home, he have some problems to. I believe that Marijuana should be legalized and taxed, as well as online gambling. This will only give the government more money and the people a better country. We will ensure that you are safe when you are anywhere in the country. Americans must and will feel safe in and out of their homes. The relationship between the people and our law enforcement needs to improve. We will help build trust by making police wear body cameras. Finally, our country will return to the moon and be far more involved in Science.

From another country's perspective, we are pretty weak. Russia and China and North Korea and Iran do many things that basically tease America and their message of "we're better than you" seems to be true when it isn't. I will do whatever is necessary to prove the rest of the world and Americans that we are the greatest, strongest, biggest, and best country in the entire world and you can't do these types of things to us and expect nothing to occur. China manipulates its currency while Russia expands their territory trying to make us take the bait in both Ukraine and in Syria while Iran is getting Billions of dollars from us and basic access to Nukes... they don't need us to survey their facilities because with the amount of money we gave them, they can buy their own nuclear weapons! This all happens while their government shouts "death to America" and North Korea threatens our allies.

Smaller countries or groups such as ISIS are taking control of the Middle East and we keep falling for the bait of other countries and our current flawed leaders would probably go to war in the Middle East... for the third time and most likely need to spend many lives, dollars, and time to basically get nothing. We can't do anything really that will work unless we do what I proposed: A small amount of highly skilled military members to be sent in as ground troops and take them out and replace them every 6 months. If we do this and continue airstrikes except at a higher rate, ISIS should be eliminated within two years and if we then take out the Iranian President, Syrian President, and restore territory and homes and a democracy to the Middle East, we should be able to re-stabilize the Middle East. Our nation will also continue support for Israel. Our "Free Trade" plans are nowhere near free trade and free enterprise. Instead, it's just other countries yet again taking advantage of America. And you may not hear about this one often but our allies are not paying their fair share. Japan, Canada, Italy, Turkey, France, Germany, Mexico, and other allies don't help as they should. We can not let it continue...

Below is my idea for a military partnership between Russia, the U.S., and China.

We will create an alliance between Russia, China, and the United States. These nations would fight and conquer whatever was diplomatically necessary. These nations, with their extreme military power, would aid us in fights against terrorism, and would be a good alliance.

This alliance would be for militaristic purposes only. It will cause all 3 nations to spend ⅓ of what they would have to if they conquered the subject on their own. The majority of the 3 nations must agree to the policy or plan if all 3 nations are to work together on it.

This alliance would last 10 years and may be renewed after expiration. The alliance will help us renew relationships and help the 3 superpowers remain superpowers rather than the 3 superpowers going against each other and causing the 3 nations and the world to suffer. Meetings will be held monthly between the 9 members of the URC council (3 will be appointed by each nation). 5 of the 9 members of the council must agree if the three nations are to perform the action being voted on. Every year the President's of each nation will meet. The location of the meeting will alternate each year (United States, China, or Russia). This relationship will be beneficial to all 3 nations as well as the world.

Below is a basic blueprint for what will happen in the first year of my administration.

My first year in office would consist of the most changes. These changes will reform America to our well deserving prosperous state. During my first year in the Oval Office, we will...

- Do all we can to end illegal immigration, with a very sophisticated system with expansion of 21st century technology
- Eliminate Sanctuary Cities (Day 1)
- All immigrants will learn English before being accepted into the U.S. (System/Law implemented Day 1)
- Eliminate our "First come first serve" border system and replace it with a totem poll. If you can contribute more to society, you will be admitted before

someone who can't (System/Law implemented Day 1)

- Expansion of border patrol agents (10,000) (First Week)
- Deportation force (10,000 people) (1st Month)
- Give enough money to Flint, Michigan for them to fix the water crisis in a year (Day 1)
- Repeal and rewrite Affordable Care Act (Day 1)
- Place a maximum capacity on magazines (First Month)
- Have U.S. health experts create a psychological test for future gun buyers to take
- Allow concealed carry nationwide (First Month)
- Eliminate "Gun Free Zones" (First Month)
- Spend another $100 Billion on U.S. Military
- Eliminate Common Core Standards (1st Month)
- Meet with Kim Jong Un
- Have a meeting with both Putin and Xi Jinping at the same time (First 6 Months)

- Eliminate Social Security (for all who don't currently reap its benefits)
- Ban abortion after 3 months (First Month)
- Stop federally funding the abortion part of Planned Parenthood (Day 1)
- Move towards equal pay
- Make election day a national holiday (Day 1)
- Raise federal minimum wage to $10
- Get all physically and mentally capable people off welfare.
- Lower Corporate Income Tax to 20% (First Month)
- People who deny a job will not receive welfare (Law implemented Day 1)
- Legalize and tax online gambling and marijuana (1st Month)
- Term limit of 4 years for Congress (1st Month)
- People on "No-Fly List" can't buy gun (1st Month)
- Eliminate state lines for healthcare (Day 1)
- All law enforcement will need to wear body cameras
- Officially declare war with ISIS (First Month)

- Much More Miscellaneous Items…

Below is what I believe and hope the future of America will look like after my election.

The future of America is at a tipping point. Assuming i'm elected to the presidency, a huge page will turn in our history that will give us prosperity and restore greatness to everyday Americans. Everyone will be awoken and we will be the #1 Global Superpower and every country in the world will know America is back and better than ever before!

If elected, our border will be secured futuristically. Illegal immigration will no longer be a threat and illegals currently in the country will be dealt with depending on the scenario but we will ensure that illegals are overall no longer a true issue. Our border force will be superior to all other countries as well as our border technology. At the border, America will be #1.

Another important issue is guns. Gun magazines will have a maximum capacity of 16. Concealed carry will not only be allowed nationwide but encouraged. All "Gun Free Zones" will be eliminated and an armed official will be placed at each one of these places. A psychological test will be made for future gun owners and overall, the very small threat of guns will be much much smaller and gun ownership will be encouraged.

Our foreign policy will be amazing. I will work together with so many other leaders of other countries and even ones that we don't work with. I will want to meet with Kim Jong Un, as well as Putin and Xi Jinping very quickly. Our military will be expanded extremely but we will withdraw from many places where we are not immediately threatened. In all non domestic bases, we will cut deployment in half. By the end of my first term, we will have two new airplanes, with a fleet of 200. We will have a new submarine with a fleet of 10. Also, a new navy ship with a fleet of 25 and a new helicopter with a fleet of 100. Our military will be so large we won't need to use it rather than so small we can't use it. We will formally declare war with ISIS and defeat them by the end of my first term. NATO will pay their fair share and we will remain a member. China will be put where it belongs on the totem pole and we will help refugees find refuge elsewhere such as in Saudi Arabia where they literally have 100,000 empty and vacant tents they could use equipped with full electricity but never house them here. As I have said many times, it's very risky and we can't take a risk right now. We will still help them but they have so many other places they could go for refuge and as we saw with Germany, it didn't really work out very well.

Economically, we will help promote business growth by lowering the corporate income tax to 20%. We will get people who are currently mentally and physically well off of welfare and if they deny a job, they will no longer receive welfare. We will put a limit on how long people can receive welfare with the exception of children related benefits. The fraudulent Social Security program will be eliminated. People who haven't put any money into Social Security won't need to deal with it and will never put a penny into it and people who have put money in will receive their promised pensions. The federal minimum wage will be raised to $10. We will lower tax rates on income brought over sea so we can get the $2 Trillion companies have offshore back here which would be beneficial to both parties. Our unemployment rate would go below 1%, our GDP will rise, and overall, economically, we will thrive and surpass China and all other countries in the economic world.

Here at home we will legalize and tax "sins" like marijuana and online gambling. Congress members will begin to have term limits of 4 years. The Affordable Care Act will be partially repealed and replaced. Law enforcement will need to wear body cameras to give definitive answers. We will return to space and get scientifically involved much more so our country can thrive and our movement will succeed.

Below are some very good quotes on an array of issues.

- "Coming here illegally doesn't make you any more of an immigrant than breaking

into someone's house makes you part of
their family."
- "Being offended doesn't make you
right."
- "Saying pistol grips make guns more
dangerous is like saying race stripes
make my prius go faster."
- "If Kaepernick refuses to stand for the
national anthem to protest racial
inequality then will he refuse to take his
paycheck to protest income inequality?"
- "In 1776, our country's greatest leaders
led us and they haven't been seen
since."
- "Welfare's goal should be to end its
existence, rather than expand its
existence."
"The other day I saw a sign, it said
"please don't feed the birds, feeding
creates a dependent population. That is
a potential health hazard and creates a
costly mess and I asked why this logic
isn't used in our society."
- "Ever wonder how the Federal Reserve
works? Just look at rule #11 of
Monopoly. It says "Some players think
the bank is bankrupt if it ever runs out of
money. The bank never goes bankrupt.

To continue playing, use slips of paper to keep track of each player's banking transactions until the bank has enough paper money to operate again. The banker may also issue "new" money slips on slips of ordinary paper." That's what the average person would call corrupt."

- "When you lie to the government, it's a felony but when the government lies to you, it's called politics."
- "Good people don't need laws that tell them how they should act and the bad people don't care about those laws and the worst people of all, the politicians, always find a way to write those laws."
- "Capitalism distributes unequal amounts of wealth while socialism distributes an equal amount of poverty."
- "If the Cigarette Tax is meant to stop people from smoking than the Income Tax is meant to stop people from working."

Here are just some of the many effects of my administration will have.

- Borders would be secure and the growing number of people who come here legally would drastically improve our economy.
- Mass shootings would drastically decrease and the ones that do exist wouldn't result in as many casualties.
- Our military would be far more technologically advanced than ever before.
- ISIS's locations in Iraq and Syria would disappear within 2 years, although we will keep using our system there for an additional 2 years since they most likely will return.

- We would stop policing the world as much as we do today.
- Common Core would be eliminated so more Billions of dollars will be available for states and the failed and wrong system will go away.
- The possibility of voter fraud would be eliminated entirely.
- The salary gap between men and women will fall drastically meaning theoretical equal wages would exist. (even though they are already basically equal)
- Greenhouse gas related health concerns would be basically eliminated and the U.S. would "go more green."
- Minimum wage workers would make more money.
- Many people will no longer need welfare and wouldn't be dependent on it.
- Americans would make about 10% more each year and they would pay less in taxes.
- Corporations would hire many more workers every year so economy grows and unemployment rate falls.
- Less people will be on drugs.

- Veterans would be taken care of more than they currently are.
- Americans that need it will receive temporary health insurance.
- Fatal shootings done by officers or directed towards officers would happen less often.
- The U.S. would return to space and learn and study it. This should benefit our lives in the near future.
- America's National Debt would be eliminated within 8 years. If we kept doing this after 8 years, other countries will have debt with us and we would receive trillions in a surplus.
- Much more prosperous proposals...

Chapter 7
Views

"Be sure to put your feet in the right place, then stand firm." -Abraham Lincoln

Below are some of the views of I have in regards to certain subjects in the state of California

California has the opportunity to be the greatest state in America, and it should be. We have so much money but people that don't know how to spend it correctly. We have so many problems and people that don't know how to fix it. That's where I come along... and here's how we fix it.

Immigration

- It is estimated that about 6.5% of California's population consists of illegal immigrants. That's about 2.5 Million people! We will have an expansion of border patrol and have a fleet of drones that survey the border, monitor everything, and provide us evidence to use to help us find and catch them.
- The whopping 82 Sanctuary Cities in the state of California will no longer exist. Illegal Immigration is under federal jurisdiction but the federal government doesn't mandate the fact that illegal

immigration is under federal jurisdiction... and this is how sanctuary cities were created. The fact that they exist is troublesome and as we see in San Francisco and many other sanctuary cities, lives could be saved if they didn't exist. During my first day as governor, I will end sanctuary cities across California and stop funding them. More in "California Immigration Plan".

- We will focus mainly on the number of illegal immigrants currently in California and use a fleet of drone surveillance to help combat the new problems that we face at our border daily.
- Don't pay a penny to illegal immigrants which cost our citizens $25 Billion annually.

<u>Economy</u>

- Statewide minimum wage is currently $10. The average cost of living in California is currently $12.34 an hour. If we raised the minimum wage to $15, inflation would be crazy. If we incrementally raised the minimum wage to $12.50, people could afford to live in the Golden State and inflation wouldn't be drastic or detrimental to everyone else. This is a perfect Median to the extremely high $15 and the Extremely low $10.

- The current sales tax rate in California is 7.5% at the state level and a maximum of 2.5% at a local level. This will be changed to 6% at the state level and a maximum of 1.5% at a local level. This would allow the highest possible sales tax rate to be 7.5%.
- The current income tax in California varies from 1% to 13.3%. There are also a total of 9 tax brackets in California. We need simplification in this system. There will only be 4 tax brackets and a maximum tax rate of 10%. More info is located in my tax plan.
- California has the 14th highest unemployment rate, at 5.5%. We will bring this number down to 4% within 4 years.
- We have some of the largest seaports in the world and they are the most secure ones to. We have the innovative Silicon Valley and the epicenter of bio-technology known as San Diego. Yet we can't figure a way to take advantage of this. We will...

Healthcare

- Rising rates, the detrimental costs for both people and the government, and lack of transparency are just some of the problems in California's healthcare system. This can and will be solved.

Education

- Change the mandated age for Kindergarten from 6 to 5. Notable studies show that if you start school at a younger age, you will have a far better life, far better results, more likely to take AP classes, etc.
- Increase funding for K-12 schools by 16.5%. (state level)
- We have the highest student to teacher, student to counselor, student to librarian, and student to administrator ratios in the country. This must and will stop as we will hire another 200,000 teachers and administrators to public schools across the state.
- Innovate school technology and infrastructure.
- Fire all current "underprepared" or "novice" teachers who make up about 6% of California's teachers. Rehire new

teachers who aren't incompetent at
teaching the next generation.

Infrastructure

- We are going to fund the hell out of the
infrastructure sector and we will
increase the current $10 billion annual
budget devoted to infrastructure to $60
billion each year. Were going to make
sure this money isn't just getting thrown
around either.
- Fix all current infrastructure that needs
to be fixed within two terms as
Governor.

Crime

- Expand "drug courts" in California. 49%
of people who participated in drug
courts repeated criminal activity as to
65% who didn't go to drug courts and
repeated criminal activity.
  - Quadruple the amount of camera
  monitoring/surveillance statewide.
- Deport criminals in our jails at once a
well as illegal immigrants we end up
catching in police confrontations. If they
don't break the law or have contact with
law enforcement, we won't go find them
but if they do, bye bye.

- Ensure former offenders receive a job. Studies show prisoners who received a job within the first two months of being released had a far less chance of repeating criminal activities then those who were unemployed after the first two months.
- More in "California Crime Reform".

Social

- Ban abortion statewide after 3 months.
- Legalize and tax marijuana statewide for recreational use and legalize and tax online gambling.
- Make Election Day a statewide holiday.
- Pass law that automatically registers you to vote when you renew your California driver's license.
- Bring unemployment rate to under 3%

Drought

- This is a subject the current administration has no idea on how to handle. They are almost entirely to blame for the existence of the dreadful and detrimental California drought.
- It all starts with a total lack of rain, but it is important to recognize the fact that there is nothing we can do that will help this, even if the cause is "climate

change". We can't produce more rain by spending more money and creating more regulations.

- Mandatory Drip Irrigation on all agricultural land. This would drastically help the drought as far more effective watering methods must be enacted and regulated.
- Offer $5 per square foot of land that is Xeriscaped in all of California.
- Open a Water Recycling plant in every California water district.
- Put water desalination in 10 major California cities (within two years). Those cities will be Los Angeles, San Diego, San Jose, San Francisco, Fresno, Sacramento, Long Beach, Oakland, Bakersfield, and Anaheim.

Guns

- Allow concealed carry statewide.
- Repeal the ban of "assault rifles".
- Hire 12,000 armed officials and put them into public schools in California.
- Create a psychological test gun owners and gun buyers need to pass to get a gun.
- The Second Amendment is your permit to own a gun, and it doesn't expire. In

other words, end the need for a permit
to have a gun.

Chapter 8
Economics

"The best investment you can make is in
yourself" -Warren Buffett

Below are some economic policies I have in
mind for the state of California.

California's economy is ranked 7th in the world.
We have many people and many hard working
people but the number of people who are
unemployed is on the rise. Our labor
participation rate is high and overall, our

economy is fine, if not excellent but it can be better and it will be...

My goal of this plan is to mainly get people on the same page. Right now, most the people who are unemployed are unemployed since they don't have the skills needed to get the jobs that are being offered. We don't want this to continue so we will ensure high schools and community colleges are on the same page and ensure that graduates have the opportunity to succeed. We will also try to make sure that people who don't have a job, and especially those on welfare, start succeeding soon.

We will create a limit for how long a Californian can stay on welfare. This limit will be one year. We will also improve communications and training to ensure every welfare recipient will be trained to the level they need to get a job and if they decline the job, that's their fault. We will raise the minimum wage over time. It will eventually reach $12.50.

Simplification of our tax system will also help both parties. Only 4 tax brackets will be implemented and taxes will be lowered for most. Overall, our economy is fine but with these policies, our economy will flourish and our GDP should exceed that of France and maybe even the United Kingdom making our GDP the 5th highest in the world. These policies also support a lower unemployment rate and that number should be under 4% which would make our statewide unemployment rate the 10th lowest in the country. These policies would stimulate economic growth and must be followed if we want our economy to succeed.

Here is my proposed tax plan for the state of California.

Annual Income	Current Tax Rate	Future Tax Rate
Under $30,000	1-4%	2.5%
$30,000-$60,000	6-9.3%	5%
$60,000-$250,000	9.3%	8%
Over $250,000	9.3-12.3%	10%

I will eliminate all deductions and loopholes for the income tax so no one can essentially evade paying, no matter the circumstances.

Annual Corporate Income	Current Tax Rate	Future Tax Rate
Over $0	8.84%	5%

I will eliminate loopholes and deductions for the corporations as well. Far too many corporations get away with paying

Current Sales Tax	Future Sales Tax
7.5%	5%

I will pass a law that lowers the state level sales tax to 5% from the current and absurdly high 7.5%.

This is my proposed budget for the state of California

15 Billion from Corporate Income Tax
95 Billion from Income Tax
30 Billion from Sales Tax
10 Billion from License Tax
50 Billion from Special Funds
5 Billion from Marijuana and Online Gambling Tax
6 Billion from Other
General Fund: 216 Billion from 220 Billion

Pensions: 25 Billion from 40 Billion
Drought: 6 Billion from 0
Health Care: 20 Billion from 50 Billion
Education: 70 Billion from 60 Billion
Welfare: 10 Billion from 20 Billion
Transportation: 25 Billion from 10 Billion
Infrastructure: 30 Billion from 2.5 Billion
Government: 7.5 Billion from 7.5 Billion
Protection: 15 Billion from 15 Billion
Interest: 7.5 Billion from 7.5 Billion
Total: 216 Billion 210 Billion

Below is my plan to end the debt in California.

The answer to solving our $400 Billion statewide debt is actually very simple. All we need to do is have everyone over the age of 18 pay $2,500 annually for 8 years. The average income in California is $61,500 so on average, this will be a 4% tax. Our debt will be eliminated in 8 years. Then, we need to ensure our debt doesn't grow or redevelop. We will do this by mandating our spending and giving people a voice.

$2,500 is a simple solution but the mandating isn't. I've already addressed the fact that we will spend about $10 Billion each year on our interest alone regardless. If we don't try to eliminate the "wall of debt", that number will continue to rise detrimentally and eventually, we won't be able to recover without very serious problems. The $2,500 will bring in about $53 Billion each year. 100% of this will go to our debt. Our debt will be eliminated if we do this and stop overspending, and this is possible.

We stop overspending by simply being competent. We will allow the people to have a say. If we are going to spend a penny more than we have that fiscal year, the people will get a say and will have the opportunity to overturn and therefore make us rewrite the budget. This will give our representatives incentives to spend money how it should be spent. This is all so simple yet nobody has solved it... That stops today.

This is my plan to fix our infrastructure in California.

California has some very serious infrastructure problems that need to be solved in the very near future. These problems are caused by current and past administrations that don't know what the they're doing. I will fix these problems.

California's current representatives haven't addressed a very important issue: Infrastructure. They may address it but nobody has felt stronger on it then me. I think it is essential that our roads, bridges, tunnels, airports, schools, etc. remain in adequate condition and I believe we should expand in innovation. We should aspire to be great and our infrastructure should be the greatest in the country, rather than 34th.

It is estimated that we need about $20 Billion in infrastructure funding each year to fix our infrastructure problems within two terms as governor. Our public transportation is horrible and i'm sure we all remember the $100 Billion bullet train project that was disastrous, behind schedule, and won't work for a long time, and even when it is, it's insufficient. It's too late to fix any of that since construction is already underway and the money is already taken out of your pockets but it shouldn't have happened in the first place.

Anyways, in California, half of our dams our hazardous, 12% of our bridges are structurally deficient, there are $46 Billion in water infrastructure needs annually, $4 Billion needed for park funding, $20 Billion needed to fix our roads, $25 Billion needed to fix our schools, $1.5 Billion annually needed to fix our wastewater systems, and in order to fix it all in eight years, we would need at least $50 Billion each year. It can and will happen, here's how.

First, we will increase our current state budget devoted to Infrastructure. It is currently about $5 Billion and we will raise it to $31 Billion. We will also raise the current portion of the state budget devoted to public transportation from the current $9 Billion to $19 Billion. Specific spending listed below but basically we're going to fix what needs to be fixed and expand current projects and create new ones to innovate California.

ANNUAL BUDGET: $55 Billion
NEEDED TO BE FIXED: $440 Billion
YEARS TO FIX IT: 8

Type Of Infrastructure	Future Annual Spending	Years Needed To Fix
Aviation	$500 Million	8
Water	$6 Billion	8
Levees	$3.5 Billion	8
Ports	$1.5 Billion	8
Solid Waste	$10 Billion	8

Transportation	$25 Billion	8
Urban Runoff	$8.5 Billion	8
Wastewater	$5 Billion	8

We will begin to see incremental growth in our infrastructure if we follow this plan for the next 8 years and elect the only person who will implement this plan for the next 8 years (me).

Chapter 9
California Plans

"You have to think anyway, so why not think big?" -Donald Trump

---

The below plan is my plan for immigration reform in California.

Immigration in California is a very controversial topic but it shouldn't be. Illegal Immigration is very damaging to California and to the country and even it's people. Immigration should be encouraged but instead, with our current system, you're better off coming here illegally and receiving our benefits and housing we offer. We shouldn't reward criminals and their families and we no longer will...

California is a large state with a large amount of people, 40 million to be exact, but a number that isn't exact is the number of illegal immigrants currently in California. One thing however is certain and that is the fact that the number of illegal immigrants here in California is at least 2.5 million or 6.5% of our population. 70% of these illegal immigrants come from our neighbor: Mexico.

We need to first do as much as we can to stop more illegals from coming here. We will do that by using technological advancements, drones in particular as well as sensors that would help us develop a sophisticated monitoring system. The next step after this is to deal with the ones we have. The 2.5 million people who are illegal in California will be asked to step forward for evaluation. In order to pass the "evaluation", they will need to have no criminal record. The estimated 20% of illegal immigrants in California with a criminal record will not qualify for permanent residency and will therefore be deported. We will also have a drug test when they go through the "evaluation" Next, we have the educated. If they have a high school diploma, they can stay and if they don't, they need to get one if they want to stay. It is estimated that 40% of the illegal immigrant population in California has a high school diploma.

This leaves us with roughly 1 million currently illegal immigrants. If they would like to have permanent residency, they must pay taxes and the second they stop paying taxes or are criminally charged, they will be deported. Other than that, they're good to go and we will give them permanent residence. This will make them almost equal to you except for the fact they will be unable to vote.

Finally, we have Sanctuary Cities. They are terrible and have caused many deaths of innocent people. They are a magnet for illegal immigration and justify the crime and therefore, all 70 Sanctuary Cities in California should be eliminated. If we follow all of the policies listed in this plan, our border will stay advanced and safe, as will you and your family and law abiding currently illegal immigrants will have a path to permanent residency and the immigration system will be fixed.

This is my plan for the future of education in California.

Our children are being set back by government run education. We don't do anything to prevent or help this. K-12 schools aren't funded enough. 6% of our teachers are classified as "underprepared" or "novice" and must be laid off immediately. Our student to teacher ratio is extremely high and we must hire another 200,000 teachers who are capable of doing the job. We will take education out of Washington and we will fund education 16.5% more annually ($10 Billion) at the state level. If we don't do this and much much more, our K-12 education system will stay ranked 40th in the nation or maybe even lower.

About 83% of Californians believe our education system is problematic and I haven't heard a single efficient solution to the problem. About ⅓ of our state budget is spent on education and schools as well as school districts rely heavily on the money the state provides. Many of our students are in "reliance". 54% of them are on free or reduced lunch and 25% of them don't even speak fluent english, the language of our land.

Our student to teacher ratios are 26-1, much higher than the 15-1 state average. We will solve this problem by first hiring more teachers and faculty members, 200,000 to be exact. This would cut our ratio in half, making it 13-1. This would be beneficial to our future, AKA our children, to the schools and school districts, and to the government.

Next, about one in every 10 students in California will drop out of High School and another one in ten will not pass High School. That means one in every 5 students will not get a High School Diploma, something that is essential to success. We need to literally make this impossible and we will. We will make High School mandatory in California rather than allowing individuals to drop out when they turn 18. We will also allow children to be educated at a younger age making Kindergarten available to children aged 4 and older by the first day of school. We will also stop making schools gun free zones, as well as every other place in California. We will also make sure there is at least one armed official at each public school in California and this will prevent school shootings and lower the fatalities associated with them. If we follow all the plans listed above, our educational system will thrive!

This is my plan for healthcare in California.

California's Health Care problem is a lesser known issue but it effects everyone. 30% of people in California receive Medicaid or Medical benefits. Californians pay about $7,000 per person each year in healthcare services. These services amount to $75 Billion annually in the state budget alone which is about 37% of the state budget. We need reformation!

California has more people than any other state and therefore needs to have greater leadership than anywhere else in the country so we can take care of all of our people only at a far more affordable rate and when I say affordable, I'm not talking Obama affordable... I'm talking affordable for the people and the government, and this is possible.

Premiums are rising on average about 40% in California. Last year, 20% of Californians reported they didn't go to a doctor because of the price. Medical costs have doubled over the last 10 years and the state of our Healthcare system is disastrous and our elected representatives aren't committed to lowering these rates or the number of people on Medicaid. Instead, they simply put more and more money into a terrible system that needs to, and will be, fixed.

We will drastically defund Medicaid. It's extremely high $50 Billion annual cost will be lowered to a $20 Billion annual cost. We will no longer support reliance on welfare at any point in time. We then will reform the insurance regulations that are the pure cause of higher rates. Lack of transparency, lack of doctors, the raise of rates, and terrible financial management are the huge problems in California's Health Care system and they will all be solved if we follow this plan.

Below is my plan for crime reform in California.

Violent crime rates in California's 15 largest counties rose on average 10% in 2015 and rose about the same percent on a statewide level. Property crime also rose in those same counties an average of about 6% and about 5% on the state level last year. Overall, crime is on the rise... and it shouldn't be. Whoever commits these crimes, of any kind, whether they be misdemeanors, felonies, etc. should be punished and punished fairly. Our current judicial system punishes second time drug users more than rapists or murderers, which is wrong. We will fix the problems associated with our judicial system and we will also lower violent crime rates

One crime that is committed on a large scale level in California is illegal immigration. The vast majority of these illegals come from the neighboring country known as Mexico. It is estimated that about 7% of California's 40,000,000 residents are illegal. Despite only accounting for 7% of the population in the state of California, they account for 13% of the population in California's prisons. About 15,000 illegals are in our prisons and as governor, I will demand their deportation as well as their monitoring within my first week. It also doesn't help when all of the sanctuary cities in California rank in the top 20 for crime rates per 1,000 citizens. We will also have much higher security at our border to prevent further illegal immigration…if you would like to see my more in depth plan for this, go to my California Immigration page.

Crime isn't the only problem. The real problem is the amount of money we spend on these criminals. We spend about $10 Billion each year on prisoners or about $65,000 per inmate each year. We only spend about $10,000 per student each year. This means we put 6.5 times as much money into people who broke the law compared to people who are still learning the laws and attempting to be nothing like the prisoners. We will cut funding to prisoners and prisons and raise funding for our future. We will cut spending by 80% to prisoners. The new cost per prisoner will be about $13,000. This will make California the lowest cost per inmate state in the nation.

Illegal immigration isn't the only crime committed on a large scale in California. Property crime is extremely popular in California. 1 in 40 people in California commit property crime. This is about 2.5% of the population or about 1 Million cases each year. As Governor, I will double the minimum fees as well as sentences for property crimes such as petty theft, burglary, or vehicle theft.

We will totally reform sentencing in California. 90% of inmates in California have been there before and were returning. This is because California has absolutely horrible rehabilitation processes and programs. It's an epidemic in all of America. We are so worried about some guy getting caught with an ounce of Marijuana and we continue to try to criminalize it at such an extreme cost. This paves way for a black market. This also paves way for overdoses. I'm not pro total decriminalization, but I am pro efficiency… and this isn't efficient. We spend roughly $57 a second to fight drugs. The war on drugs has been a total failure and by definition, it is insanity… AKA, doing the same thing repeatedly but expecting a different result. We will no longer spend this vast amount of money to fight drugs and will invest our money in the right areas to ensure that California is made efficient as it was before.

These are my plans regarding guns in California.

Liberals have taken our great state over. I'm not saying conservativeness is the other way to go, i'm just saying liberals sure as hell aren't the right way to go. What we need is honesty. Taking away rights isn't going to help get guns away from people who will use them to cause harm. Good people don't need laws to tell them what to do and bad people don't care about the laws. They will always find a way to get a gun. The idea assualt weapons are bad is simply because of a great branding campaign. "Assault Weapons" accounted for 3% of murders over the last 5 years nationwide… 3 times as many murders were the results of hands and feet. Although it is true that assault weapons or more so semi automatic weapons do more damage when used, they are rarely used.

We will allow concealed carry without a permit. The Second Amendment is your permit to own a gun and that permit never expires. We however will ensure that the people who get these guns are non-violent and mentally stable. We will have a psychological test we will make each person who attempts to buy a gun go through.

We will repeal the ban on "assault weapons". Last year, our gun statistics showed that our "death by assault weapons" were the 10th highest by state in the country. We had 3.4 deaths by assault weapons per 100,000 people. Idaho has no regulation on assault weapons yet they had 0.8 deaths by assault weapons per 100,000 people. Also, California's statewide gun ownership is about 20% and Idaho's gun ownership is about 57%. It is like this in many other states as well and it proves we should encourage gun ownership in response to gun violence.

We will put over 12,000 armed officials in California public schools. These people will be a member of a union that is supported by the state. The people in this union will need to be trained and pass certain tests and the safety of your children will be ensured.

Overall, guns have been a very debatable topic yet the resolution is very simple. It is a fact that more guns equals more safety. Higher gun ownership equals lower gun murder rates. We should encourage gun ownership and make sure that those gun owners are suitable to own those guns. If we follow this plan, our gun violence rates will go down and we will be protected by more than a phone.

Below is my plan to end the current drought in California.

Unless you've been living under a rock, you are well aware of the fact that California is in a drought. Our current administration created this drought and is the reason it still exists. My plan will put an end to the drought and ensure efficiency and productivity when it comes to our water and our water systems.

We will start by evolving our irrigation technology. About 43 million acres are used for agriculture in California. The water management at these places are terrible. We will force all places used for agriculture to use drip irrigation. This will save us about 5 million gallons of water each year and not cost us a penny.

Next, we will use much more rain runoff systems. This is simple and cost effective. This will save California about 0.5 million acre feet of water each year. We will also offer $5 per square foot of land xeriscaped. Xeriscaping will save us about 1 million acre feet of water each year. Desalination plants will also be opened and used. We will install 5 of these each year, costing us about $2 Billion each year. This will save us about 0.5 million acre feet of water each year. What will help us the most is mandatory drip irrigation. With 21st century efficiency in our agricultural systems, we will save about 5 million acre feet of water each year. Since our current deficiency is about 6.5 million acre feet per year, or 2.2 Trillion gallons of water each year. We will begin to have a surplus within 4 years with innovative technology and we will once and for all end our water deficiency.

This doesn't mean the drought is fixed, it just means we will be able to save more water to help contribute to end that drought. To end the drought within 4 years, we must do many different things and we must do them efficiently and effectively. Right now, we need to get about 11 trillion gallons of water to end the drought... this won't be easy, but it won't be impossible either. The previously listed plans will produce about another 9 trillion gallons of water over the span of four years. This means we only need about another 2.2 trillion gallons of water over 4 years, or about 550 billion gallons of water each year. This can be found in multiple ways, but the most efficient and effective would be cloud seeding. Cloud seeding can increase precipitation and is a true technological and 21st century innovation. It is also very cost effective. The cost to increase precipitation rates effectively where they need to be increased varys. It will cost about $3 Billion to DOUBLE our current annual rainfall and with our rainwater recyclers, this will only give us even more water than the water that is given. This annual cost, along with the others, and along with the plans will effectively and efficiently end our drought within four years.

Chapter 10
Closing Statement

"Give all the power to the many, they will oppress the few. Give all the power to the few, they will oppress the many." -Alexander Hamilton

---

I believe that America has the potential to be so amazing... it is amazing right now but we can make it so much better. We can make breakthroughs in science, we can make our economy so large, we can lower the unemployment rate so low that less than 1% of Americans are unemployed. We can change the tax code so that everyone pays a fair proportional amount and eliminate loopholes so people don't find a way to legally pay no income tax. We can stop being so inefficient with our money. We can finally create a surplus and eliminate our National debt. We can change the healthcare system so that way premiums don't rise upwards of 100% at times. We can change the educational system so that students are invested in and education will become localized rather than federalized. We can fix our crumbling infrastructure so our water will be drinkable in places like Flint and we will be able to drive on our roads and our street lights will work. We can reform the criminal justice system so that people are punished much more fairly. We can fix our system and we can put our nation back to work. We can end disastrous trade deals. We can lower inflation. We can make our military so large that we don't have to use it rather than so small that we can't use it. We can create so much money and stop taxing corporations out of business. We can end illegal immigration and subsidization of illegal immigrants. We can stop allowing hazardous chemicals/ingredients to be put in our food that we give to our children. We, together, can make the future of America free, safe, and prosperous but only with someone who has the stance to lead.

Index

Seek Something Better
By Parker Bono

Also By Parker Bono

The Stance To Lead

As always,
I dedicate this book to the American
people and those who fight and fought
for my rights.

Contents

STATE

Introduction

The Stance To Get Elected is a book that is about the essence of winning, but particularly in elections. In the book, I explain how I plan to run my campaign, gather funds, and how to win the presidency. I also tell how I plan on getting elected as Governor of Pennsylvania. Finally, I also explain how you yourself can get involved politically.

If one is to get elected to these positions, they must have many aspects but the most important ones are a background, name recognition, and love from the people.

I will achieve a background in Politics as that will be my job for the rest of my life. I will be a public servant. I will be loved by the people as I will do what is right. I will grow, develop, and improve whatever city I reside upon as a city council member and mayor. I also will help the district in which I represent in the House Of Representatives. I will also run an excellent campaign to be governor of the state I am a resident of and ultimately win the people's vote and be elected President of the United States in 2040. This plan is outlined in this book, as well as how I shall achieve the plans.

I decided to write this book since I love politics and I have a plan for everything. I capitalize on every situation, and you should to. This book means a lot to me, and it is basically a blueprint for my future, as well as our country. I explain how I plan on winning and I also explain how we as a country will as well. You don't have to win in politics to be a winner. Millions of Americans may not be winners yet but if they have the mindset of one, they surely will be soon.

I believe everyone has something in life to give and I would love to see everyone reach their potential. I however have seen many very talented and brilliant people not do what they are easily capable of. This is called laziness. The trait of laziness has a direct correlation to failure. This book explains how to win, as well as how I plan on doing it in future elections, and in general. If you read this book, you will benefit as you will obtain new knowledge. You also will see my plans that I ensure you will occur successfully.

Chapter One
The Background

"I walk slowly but I never walk backward."
-Abraham Lincoln

If one is to get elected President of the United States, they must have a very good background. I myself will have graduated from Political Science Penn State University with a degree in . I then will run for City Council (2022), Mayor (2026), House of Representatives (2030), Governor (2034), and President (2040). My job throughout my life will be a public servant. I will provide the people with a government run by them. Nobody will be able to buy me out because I will do the right thing for the country. The jobs I will acquire in the beginning of my career and the jobs I get later on will have a domino effect on the next as each new job will be beneficial towards my future.

Another item I will be able to put on my resume is the fact that I will have eliminated the debt in every location and district I resided over. My eyes would next be on the U.S. National Debt. No sane person wants themselves, their spouse, and their children to each owe $61,500 just for living in the United States. I will run as a Republican throughout the course of my political career although I do have many independent views and common sense views such as enforcing law, eliminating the U.S. National Debt, job growth, etc. Basically, I will run as a Republican since I must pick one of the two major parties but I will actually be more of an independent.

To restate, I will graduate from Penn State University and I will have a career in politics. I will create a name for myself and I will become synonymous with victory. I will be an independent that successfully runs as a Republican. I believe that in the future I will have the necessary background to lead. I also believe I will win over the people, no matter my location, and I will be a political success.

Chapter Two
The Announcement

"We would all like to vote for the best man but he is never a candidate." -Kin Hubbard

---

After I create a background for myself in politics, I will announce my candidacy for President of the United States. My announcement speech will be approximately 5,000 words and will take about 45 minutes for me to read off of a teleprompter. I despise of the teleprompter but it is necessary at certain points in time to properly get your point across to the American people. My speech would be held on May 1, 2039, at Independence Hall in Pennsylvania. I should get approximately 7,500 people to show up for my speech, almost reaching the maximum capacity of Independence Hall (the place the Declaration Of Independence and the Constitution were written).

During my speech, I will speak out against my opponents and politicians in general, warn against associating with a political party, speak about ending the Federal Reserve, lay out my plan to end the National Debt within 8 years, immigration reform, my tax plan, problems with the world at the time and how I will do everything in my power to fix them, and much much more. Obviously, I can not predict the future by knowing what will happen in 22 years from now so I speak about things the way they are today. I would change this in my actual announcement speech, although it would be very similar.

Below is my speech announcing my candidacy for President of the United States.

"Thank you everyone for coming. That's a lot of people out there. Many thousands!

It is my great honor to be speaking here today at the location our nation was founded. When our nation was founded, the greatest leaders our country has ever seen came out and fought for liberty. I don't see that today. When our nation was founded, people knew their genders, people knew which bathroom to use, and people were willing to work relentlessly to form the system we have today. The system is perfect. It is the greatest thing the world has ever seen, and it is known as the American Experiment.

America was founded on the ideals that we wouldn't take anything from anyone. Britain attempted to tax us at an insane rate. In response we went to war. We were the underdogs but we won.

But this was back then. I don't see us winning as much as we should be today. We lose at trade, we lose at costs, we lose at the borders, and most importantly, we lose at the military. China is spending ¼ of what we are spending on the military yet they are growing their military at a quicker rate. Our government is one of the least efficient and effective in the world. If the federal government was put in charge of manufacturing iPhones, the price to make them would go up from $220 to $2,200, and our leaders are so stupid, they wouldn't change the price they sell it for. Our nation hasn't had a true leader since Ronald Reagan. Before than, we had Kennedy, before that, we had Lincoln, before that, we had Jackson,

before that, we had Jefferson, and the very first and greatest President of all time was George Washington. Our nation lacks any and all leadership qualities. We give away everything and don't stay firm on almost any issues.
To me, it looks like our country is being too generous with other nations and is giving everything to other countries in exchange for nothing. China can tax us whatever they want and our leaders will do nothing. Russia could opt out of a nuclear treaty and we would still remain in it by ourselves. Iran's leaders and citizens could chant "death to America" and our leaders might actually do something this time... give them about $100 Billion. It's disgraceful. Of course, all of these things actually happened, and the response of our leaders are 100% accurate.

The thing is that both Republicans and Democrats make the same mistake of idiocracy. If you identify with one of these parties, you may not be very much better than them, and if anything, you are helping them. It's called divide and conquer. If you had 100% resistance, you wouldn't succeed but if you had 50% resistance and 50% support, and some of the members of the resistance and supporters silence one another, you no longer have a full majority on either side. I am running as a Republican but I have Independent views. I would run as an Independent if it wouldn't bankrupt my political career. Sadly, in this day and age, it would.

While i'm on the subject of corrupt, evil, crooked, and horrible politicians and political systems, let me talk about the Federal Reserve. The Federal Reserve is one of the worst outputs from one of the worst administrations.

Woodrow Wilson was the most racist post civil war era presidents we have ever had. He also pulled a Bush and wrongfully got us into horrible wars that we had nothing to gain from at the cost of American taxpayers and thousands of lives.

Before I get back to the Federal reserve, let me just say, we're gonna end the draft. We will. As the great Ron Paul once stated, "If the war is worth fighting, people will volunteer".

You see, we're not sick like the rest of them. The rest of the politicians don't care what it costs, they will push their agenda at the expense of how ever many lives or how ever much cash it costs.

The Federal Reserve was meant and created to put ourselves into a plethora of debt. The Federal Reserve isn't federal. In fact, it has shareholders, and they receive a 6% annual dividend. There also are 12 banks that own the Federal Reserve. Many of these banks are international banks. International banks have power over the United States money supply. Isn't that amazing? You can go to their website and you will see it.

Everytime we ask the Federal Reserve to print money, we go deeper into debt. That's right: the U.S. Government doesn't issue a penny. If we could, we would just issue enough to pay off our debts. We however can not do that. The Federal Reserve simply prints money out of nowhere. This paper is also worth absolutely nothing. Literally nothing. It's worth the paper it's printed on. It may have numbers printed on it but that means nothing if it's not backed by anything.

I am currently working on a replacement to the Federal Reserve, until then, we will audit the Federal Reserve. Later on during the campaign, I will release my replacement plan.

Money is power, and debt is inevitable loss of that power. I don't know why other countries still let us borrow money from them. We owe $20 trillion. I'm going to end the National Debt. I will do it in 8 years if I am given the chance. I guarantee you. I will do this via a simple 3 point plan. Step one is ending all tax loopholes and abolishing some credits. Estimates say this will give about $200 Billion each year. Step two is to legalize and tax online gambling and marijuana, both at a 20% rate. Estimates show this will provide an extra $50 Billion each year. Finally, and most importantly, we will extract oil from the Green River Formation. There is about 2 Trillion barrels of extractable oil in this area. We will drill 5% of this each year, or about 100 Billion barrels each year. It will cost us about $2.5 Trillion each year to do this, but each year we will extract and sell $5 Trillion worth of oil, so we get $2.5 trillion each year. This plan will end our National Debt and create a small but still adequate surplus. After I end the National Debt, I will attempt to pass a bill or add an amendment that would force all future budgets to be equal to or less than the amount received that year in taxes. This would allow our nation to never again be in debt.

Wouldn't it be amazing if we were owed trillions and weren't forced into economic slavery? This is common sense people. No one else will say this. Republicans and Democrats alike won't say it because either they don't understand it, or they benefit from it. The elite benefit from anything, why wouldn't they benefit from this as well? I'm not saying they do, but I wouldn't throw it out.

I don't like to just talk about the bad, but you have to bring this stuff up to fix it. We lose a lot as a country. We win as well, but absolutely not as much as we should. Particularly, we lose at the immigration level. Other nation's aren't allowing refugees because they have seen what has happened to Europe. They have seen the horrors caused by some of them. I'm not saying all of them are bad, i'm not saying that at all. What I am saying is that some of them commit treacherous crimes, and set a precedent. The precedent is actually set in their country, but that's none of our business.

Anyways, Immigration is an amazing, and very encouraged thing. Our nation was founded on immigrants. These immigrants however didn't break any immigration laws when they came here. A lot of people nowadays do break laws we have in place in our country, and in exchange for breaking our laws, they ask and sometimes receive citizenship. Isn't that absurd? Now, with that being said, I kind of understand why they do it. People sit on the waiting list for 5 years to get into our country legally. Our current immigration system is horrible, in regards to speed at least. I will reform the system so that there is a que system implemented. I will allow people to come here legally quicker. There will be a maximum waiting period of 1 year for a response to your immigration application.

Let's say there are two people applying for citizenship, person A and person B. Person A is from a very safe and prosperous Dubai, and he applies for citizenship. He has a degree in college and has no criminal record. He however applied one year after person B applied, and person B does have a criminal record and is from a terror prone nation known as Iraq. Under my system, Person B would get priority over almost all. No longer will it be first come first serve. Admission into the greatest nation in the world will be exclusive to the people who have and will have the greatest potential in the world. No longer will we accept immigrants only to assist them through welfare for the rest of their life.

I also believe that we should innovate our border. The price of innovation will cost $1 Billion in taxpayer dollars, or about $10 per taxpayer. Although, we are going to create a surplus, so i'll reimburse you guys with 100% interest for it. If we implement the que system and increase funding by $1 Billion for deportations, drones/surveillance, and for border patrol agents, our border will be even more secure and Americans will be even more safe.

On the subject of money and taxpayer dollars, let me explain my tax plan. It's very simple. For the first three years, it will be a flat tax for all Americans of 20%. Nothing Less, nothing more. For corporations, it will be a 20% income tax with a 0.5% tax credit per 100,000 existing workers. Corporations will also have the opportunity to receive a tax credit of 1% for every 100,000 future employees they add. This will incentivize them to add hundreds of thousands of jobs. If they wanted to pay absolutely no income tax, they could employ 2.5 million workers, but we know that won't happen right? *laughter*. Oh, and I almost forgot, every fourth year of my administration, there will be no income tax. That's right, there will be a one year tax vacation every four years of my Presidency. Is that something you guys want? *Crowd exclaims yes*. Well, if you want that, vote for me, because I want that for you guys to. I also want that for our economy. Our economy will thrive under all years in my administration, but the economy will thrive most during the fourth year of my administration, and hopefully my eighth.

During my first year, I will add approximately 1.5 Million jobs, and during my first four years, I will add approximately 10 Million jobs. Next week I will be releasing a more detailed plan on how I plan on doing this.

The United States are the policemen of the world. We spend over $5 Billion every year on foreign aid, and for what in return? Our country shouldn't be willing to give away anything. Wwe should always try to win, and I will ensure that we will win. Even if it's just $1, we shouldn't give it away. We will cut foreign aid in half, as well as the cost. This will benefit ourselves, as well as the countries we are currently in. I however care more about our country than any other country, but there are still other humans that are being killed every day in those countries. Why don't we let the government of Syria deal with problems going on in Syria? We gain nothing if Syria becomes "Democratic" then elects another dictator in their first election after we spent $2 Trillion attempting to force democracy upon them. Our nation will prioritize America over all other countries. Of course we care about the refugees and all that but I care even more about the 50,000 homeless Veterans we have here in the U.S. I care more about the 15% of Americans that live below the poverty line. I care more about the millions of jobs being shipped overseas. I care more about the fact our economy is underperforming. I care more about the fact that U.S. companies have over

$2.5 Trillion parked overseas. By the way, we're gonna get that cash that's parked overseas flowing into our country. We're gonna get it back. The reason companies don't bring their cash here is because we have insanely unfair tax rates. Companies don't want to give up over ⅓ of what they earned just because they are a corporation, and you wouldn't want to do that either. We are going to lower the rate in which that cash sitting overseas is taxed to 10%. We will offer a 10% reduction so the company pays absolutely no tax on the money brought overseas into the U.S. if they agree to put at least 20% of it into developing new facilities, adding new jobs, etc. Assuming all companies choose the 20% path, we will have a 3% GDP growth just from that alone. Also, when they decide to add new jobs, you will benefit. No longer will companies take jobs and cash overseas at no cost. You the people have been hurt too much by this. Our economy has been hurt by it aswell.

Election Day is a very sacred day, and it should be treated as such. We will make Election Day a National Holiday. This will ensure that everyone has the time to vote. We will also pass a law that makes sure there is at least 1 polling place per square mile. This will ensure everyone can vote as they will have the day off and will be less than one square mile away from a polling place.

However, if one would like to vote, they must have an ID. This isn't racist, and as a matter of fact, I will have withdrawn the power racists, as well as anyone else, have from halting anyone from voting by forcing there to be a polling place every square mile in the U.S. You need an ID to receive welfare, why don't you need one to decide the future of welfare? You also need an ID to buy some nail polish at CVS, buy some cold medicines, donate blood, to buy cigarettes, and many other things. Do you think nail polish is more important than the future of our nation? *crowd yells no* I don't think so either.

Our nation's water supply is being damaged. You can't drink the water in Flint, and you shouldn't drink the water from most of our public water supplies either. This is because it is pumped with fluoride. It has been estimated that over 40% of American children suffer from dental fluorosis. In case you didn't know, dental fluorosis is what happens when you have too much fluoride. The most common types of fluoride in our drinking water are sodium silicofluoride and hydrofluorosilicic acid. Both of these chemicals are unpurified waste products that are known to have higher levels of contaminants like arsenic. More than 23 human studies and more than 100 animal studies have linked fluoride to brain damage. Would you feed your child something that would give them brain damage? *crowd yells no* I wouldn't either. This is why we will end water fluoridation.

Also, the EPA has classified fluoride as a chemical with "substantial evidence of developmental neurotoxicity." It is also estimated that about 99% of the fluoride in our water gets put down the drain, and therefore pumped into the environment. This is not good. Doctor William Hirzy is a former EPA scientist. He states "If you want to prevent sunburn, you don't drink suntan lotion, you put it on your skin. If you want to have the benefits of fluoride and oral health ... you put it on the surface of the tooth. You don't drink it." Water fluoridation is the first and only drug forced to the masses as forced medication with no control over dosage. This is also the last of those forced medications.

Space exploration and advancements in science are very very important to me. I feel like our civilization is not growing at the rate we could be. I want my administration to be known as "The Era Of Advancements". I will multiply NASA's budget by 5, improve the FDA, and we as a nation will advance scientifically significantly. I would love for my administration to no longer make it normal to be diagnosed with cancer in America. I want to end cancer. Eliminate it from the face of the Earth. Someone has to do it at some point. I would like for we as a nation to explore space. Manned exploration or not, I would like to do it. I would like to find alien life. That would be amazing. I absolutely believe it exists. There is no way we are alone. It is basically impossible that we are alone.

If there is evidence that I am given that shows there is extraterrestrial life out there, you better believe it will be released. I am not sure if the President is given this information or if this information exists but as I said if it does, you will know about it. I will lead of by and for the people, just like Abraham Lincoln. Any information available to me that would prove or disprove any "conspiracy theory" will be released to the public. This goes for all conspiracy theories, I don't want any Americans to feel insecure about the government. I want to fix the government because right now even I feel insecure about it.

We as a country have astronomically high drug prices. You guys are hurt from this since this means that you must pay much more for your medication than you should. We are going to open the hell out of our markets, wide open. Let the medication flow into our market, and let the prices fall.

I hate big tobacco, and i'm pretty sure the feeling is mutual. I want to eradicate big tobacco from the face of the earth, as well as eliminate the deaths associated with second hand smoke. Tens of thousands die every year because some idiot decided they wanted to pump chemicals into their lungs and exhale those chemicals into the air everyone must breathe. Most of the people that die because of the idiots are children. It's so sad. But you know what? Big tobacco doesn't care. They only care about profit. Big tobacco would rather have those children become addicted to cigarettes as well, and as long as they buy some cigarettes, they don't care if they die. We're going to make it illegal to smoke in public and we are going to raise the federal tax rate on cigarettes to $10. This will make sure that people don't even think about smoking. All of the federal tax revenue that comes from the cigarette tax will go towards ads that are anti-cigarette, help towards current smokers, and the rebuilding of communities crushed by big tobacco. Typically these communities are in poverty, so big tobacco targets them. It's so sad. It'll stop though... it'll stop.

We as a nation are divided. We have been since we were founded, but it has been getting worse lately. But you see, this is one of the beautiful things in America. I don't like division but I do like the right to have varying opinions. However, on some issues, it is just common sense. My campaign will be the common sense campaign. I will solve issues in a way that benefits the nation, no matter who is happy in the end. I would like to make everyone happy but there is always going to be an opposition to something. You can never please 100% of the people. But you know what you can do? You can do what is right for America, no matter what the pollsters say. What is right is what is right and what is wrong is what is wrong. Nothing less and nothing more. I will attempt to ensure that we are not a nation divided but in the end, I care more about the nation than I do my approval rating. I do love you guys though. Aren't you guys the best? *crowd cheers*

One topic we tend not to be divided on is education. Education is key to a successful society, and sadly our public educational system isn't doing too good compared to other nations. We are ranked 14th in education globally. Should America ever be in 14th place? *crowd yells no* I don't think so either. If we are to fix the plethora of errors in our educational system, there must be a plan... so here it is. Our public education system is from the 18th century when the vast majority of Americans were farmers and schools didn't have air conditioning. Our system shouldn't just be K-12 with long Summer breaks in the middle of all of it. A Harvard study found that if children don't receive early brain stimulation, they will not thrive in the future academically. We will make pre-school mandatory across the nation. This will help children get the early learning boost that they desperately need. To pay for this whole system, we will cut out the 12th grade. This will boost high school graduation rates, college enrollment, and employment rates and will overall benefit our country. We also will create a 4-3 educational system where you have four days of school then three days off. The amount of days kids get off of school where vary locally but we will require 210 days of mandatory instruction. This new schedule will help improve America as a whole.

We will also end property tax based education. Most states rely on property taxes to fund the educational system, but since wealthy houses are worth more so they pay more in taxes, the wealthy zip codes get better schools and therefore a better education than most. It will be up to the states to determine the amount but the amount of money taken from property taxes and put into the education system will need to be even or flat. No longer will the rich get to go to the good schools and the poor get to go to the bad schools. All schools will be good in America, it is called American exceptionalism, and our education system will be no different from the rest of America in the fact that we will be the best and excel at everything that we do! *crowd cheers*

Now it's time to tackle an area with opposition: healthcare. There are many different ideas as to how healthcare should work in America, but this idea is the most beneficial idea, at least towards the country as a whole. A person with common sense but an evil personality would say that the solution to the outrageous premium prices would be to cut sick people off of health insurance so that way only healthy people have health insurance and they don't use it, so therefore premiums will go down. This solution however doesn't work.

I want costs to go down and I don't want people to be dying in the streets. Prevention is key to this. When people notice they have a "bug" or a mere amount of back pain, they must consult help and if they don't let the illness snowball, costs for them or the insurance company will be drastically less. We must encourage early extermination of illnesses and support new medications that entirely eradicate certain diseases from America. That isn't entirely my healthcare plan but it would help bring down costs if it occurred.

If we are to fix the healthcare system, we must allow individuals and employers to opt out of the individual mandate. The employer mandate makes all companies or firms with 50 or more employees to pay for insurance for the employees. Almost 100% of people support the repeal of this as it is economically detrimental. It has caused a huge reduction in full time employment. This is bad. What is even worse is that some estimates state that that when the act is fully implemented, tens of millions of people could lose their health insurance that is sponsored by their employers. We will repeal the mandate, something most people would support, and by doing so, we will shrink the amount of money we take out of American's paychecks by about $282 Billion over the next 10 years.

I do not like the mandates we have in place, and neither does the economy. I will repeal the mandate implemented on seniors regarding Medicare. Seniors should be able to also opt out of this mandate. You kind of can opt out of Medicare right now but doing so would result in the loss of your Social Security benefits. To the average person, the people who truly are America, this is impossible to do. RIght now, ⅓ of doctors refuse to take Medicaid patients. This is due to government reimbursements. What do you think is going to happen to the Medicare patients when Medicare's rates become worse than Medicaid? I'll tell you what will happen, according to the Medicare agency, about 15% of the hospitals in America will go out of business. When something causes 15% of a sector to go out of business, that thing is very bad. If Seniors had the opportunity to opt out of Medicare, alternative solutions in private insurance companies would appear. It may not be the best at first because actually, Medicare is good economically for most American families but over time, it would work out as more and more Seniors would leave Medicare as the effects that have compounded continue to snowball and it would be overall better for Seniors. Freedom is a right given to all Americans, ALL. Freedom shouldn't just be given to those under 65, all Americans should have freedom to choose their healthcare, and in the end it is a choice.

I also am a very strong supporter of HSAs, or Health Savings Accounts. We had 50 million uninsured prior to the implementation of Obamacare and will still have 30 million uninsured after the full implementation of Obamacare. This may look good at the surface but simply making more people have more insurance in this country doesn't help. As a matter of fact, it makes it worse. Anyways, the reason we had and still will have so many people uninsured is because healthcare is extremely expensive. Obamacare has done nothing to combat this problem and has done lots to make this problem worse, at times up to 67% worse. Many different experts have come up with different solutions to the mess regarding our healthcare system but all of the solutions trace back to HSAs.

HSAs help bring the cost of healthcare down by putting individuals in charge of their healthcare. When you have to pay for your own healthcare, you will question all tests and costs that are proposed to you. Doctors and hospitals will then need to be more responsive to your needs or they will lose your business. Also, the price of certain tests will need to be affordable or no one will get them. This will help lower costs and make healthcare overall more affordable. But that's not it. Everyone will be able to use after-tax dollars to pay for HSAs. Health Savings Accounts already exist but a mere 5% of Americans use them. If every American had HSAs, the cost of healthcare would definitely go down. We are going to just this by changing the law. Currently not everyone is eligible to have an HSA. We will make it so everyone can have one. We will make it illegal to not have an HSA. You don't have to use your HSA as your primary source of healthcare, but you would be stupid not to. This is since we will make it great. We will remove all caps on the amount you can put into them, as well as your employer. We will make it so your employer must put in a certain of your salary into an HSA, and you can use it for whatever you want in regards to your medical needs. For those who make $10,000 or less per year, employers must pay 10% of the salary. For those who make $10,001 to $25,000, employers must pay 4% of the salary. For those who make $25,001 to $50,000, employers must pay 2% of the salary. For those who make $50,001 to $100,000, employers must pay 1% of their salary. For those who make more than $100,000 annually, employers must put in 0% and the worker must put in an amount they choose, they must however put some money into an HSA. This will make everyone have an HSA and the vast majority of people having one without needing to put money into it. If they do however put more money into it, they will be able to do so tax free and at the amount they choose, rather than paying a monthly payment on health insurance that most rarely use to pay for very expensive items, you can have an HSA and spend however much you want on whatever expenses you want. It's all your choice.

This plan may make me seem like I am anti business. This absolutely is not the case. I want businesses to grow. Small businesses are the foundation of our country. This is why we will encourage small business growth and development. We will do this by removing the very discouraging regulations and extremely high taxes that businesses must pay. The corporate tax rate will be lowered to 20%. We also will get the trillions that are sitting offshore back into our country, as I stated earlier. We will do this by taxing them at a 10% rate or a 0% rate, depending on what they choose to do. Small businesses will no longer be taxed out of business with the new corporate tax rate. I'll release more soon on policies I will enact that will create more jobs in my two terms than any other President in history and create more GDP growth than any other President.

Social security is horrible for everyone. Social security secures nothing but a poor life for seniors and debt for future generations. Not a good combo. A simple solution to social security is the total abolition of this system. This is basically what I will do. All Americans who have put money into social security will need to do the same for the rest of their lives, and all who currently receive benefits will get those benefits. All Americans who have not put any money into social security will not have to.

You might be asking why I want to do this. Well, the answer lies in debt, the fact we don't need the system, and government inefficiency. The U.S. Treasury owes $2.8 Trillion to the Social Security Trust Fund. To put it simply, we are spending more money than we take in while giving out guaranteed benefits that barely put retirees above the poverty line. 25% of the U.S. budget is dedicated to Social Security every year, or about $900 Billion. This is a large sum of money that is spent to keep Americans just $5,000 over the poverty level. Also, 33.3% of Americans have no other retirement savings, so the only benefits they receive will be social security benefits that will barely be enough to keep them above the poverty level. This however is the current benefits. Estimates state that by 2034, there will be a 21% reduction to social security benefits. This will make retirees just $1,000 over the poverty level.

There however is a solution. If we made it law that all employed people at age 18 and above must put at least 3.7% of their salary into a retirement savings account of their choice, the situation for them and the government would be much better. The government will no longer offer Social Security benefits when the last person that put money into social security dies and therefore will no longer need to spend Billions each year on the failed system and go Trillions deeper into debt. Anyways, the 3.7% is far less than the government gets, they get 6.2% out of your paycheck and another 6.2% from your employer. This is 12.4% of your income. The maximum amount of money this 12.4% tax can get you annually when you retire is $31,668 each year, and remember, this number will go down as time progresses. The numbers would be a lot worse for Social Security if the numbers were the same. Assume you made the average salary in America of about $33,200. If you made that money and started putting money into social security at age 18, when you retired at age 67, you would get about $13,000 per year in pensions. This is with no inflation or salary increases. Now, let's assume the you made the same amount of money but instead of putting money into social security, you put 3.7% of your $33,200 you made each year into a retirement savings account. Well, if this happened, the amount of money you saved would allow you to make about $32,500 each year, until you turned 82. This is 250% of what you got with social security, except it's ⅓ of the price. By the way, the life expectancy in America is 79, so you would be living longer than average in this scenario and still make more than you would with social security. Even if you lived until 100, something 0.02% of Americans do, you would make about $20,600 per year, 158% of what you would get with social security.

This solution is so much better and allows you to make 2.5% more every year. It's a win win win. It's a win for you as you make more when you retire and while you are working. It's a win for the government as they no longer must deal with the Trillions of dollars in debt associated with the program. Finally, It's a win for companies as they no longer must pay a large sum of money into a failed system, and now they get to put that money into the economy. Overall, we are going to do something nobody else can do properly: fix social security. The differences in our plan and the plans of everyone else is that our plan doesn't just stall the time in which social security will fail, it stops social security from failing and helps everyone out far more than any other plan would.

There will be many different arguments as to what causes climate change but it is a fact that it is occurring. I personally believe that climate change is occurring and there are things we could do to make the situation better, but it's not entirely our fault. However, for the simple fact that climate change is occurring, our nation will "go green", kind of. We don't want to regulate businesses out of business. We will not set any regulations but will trust corporations, yes i know, we shouldn't trust the corporations but hear me out, trust the corporations and see if they can hit the goal we have set: a 1% drop in CO_2 emissions. I would like for us to continue to have 1% drops every year throughout my administration. The corporations can do whatever they want to make this happen, it will be totally up to them. I believe the corporations will fulfil the goals we have set forth and if they don't, something will happen. But you guys have to realize that even CO_2 emissions aren't entirely our fault. Yes, there are things humans do that cause CO_2 emissions but some of the emissions do occur naturally. Also, the benefits of the number one contributor to CO_2 emissions, the burning of fossil fuels, far outweigh the bad. Fossil fuels are a cheap and plentiful reliable energy source that helps make modern life possible and compared to the efficiency of other energy sources, none can match. Do you like your life? *crowd yells yes* I do too. I would also like to debunk the "97% of scientists" claim. Firstly, science is not democratic. It used to be the consensus that the Earth was flat but then all it took was one individual to say that it wasn't and we soon realized it wasn't, so even if the figure was true, it means nothing really.

Secondly, if 97% of scientists believe humans are the cause of it, it has to come from somewhere. I won't go into detail about where the number originated from, it is an outdated number created falsely. Instead, since so many continue to cite the figure today, I would like to ask anyone who disagrees with me to gather the names of every scientist in the world and then get his or her stance on climate change and what the primary cause is. I guarantee you the number will not be 97%. Polls are very inaccurate, including the one's continuously cited today that claim 97% of scientists believe human cause is the primary cause of climate change. As I stated before, climate change is occurring, and there are things humans can do that would help reverse the effects, but it isn't entirely our fault. I still however will lower CO_2 emissions and try to help in the ways I can that benefit everyone, and we'll see what happens.

Ever since 9/11, national security has been a very popular topic of political discussion. I will make sure that terrorism doesn't reach the United States. I will also take the huge target off of our back by removing troops from all around the world. As sad as it is if a foreigner is hurt or killed by another foreigner, we must first worry about non-foreigners. These people are known as Americans and they matter the most to me. I care more about my country than I do about the world. I would choose Americanism over Globalism every single day, and if I am elected President, I will make sure America's prosperity is the number one priority. Anyways, my National Security plan involves growing the U.S. military.

This however doesn't have to be done through more military spending. Like I said earlier, how is it possible for other countries to grow militaristically at a faster rate than us yet spend ⅓ of what we spend? I will grow the military at no extra cost. National security nowadays is also dependent on cyber security. I will improve our country's cyber defense and ensure our grid and other cyber firms aren't vulnerable to potential attacks from the enemy. One way we also will help our country is through the foundation of the URC. The URC will be an agreement/treaty with the United States, China, and Russia, the three superpowers of the world. The URC will be a militaristic treaty only and would expire after 10 years, with the possibility of renewal. This agreement would help the U.S. as we could destroy terrorism threats much easier. I go into more detail in my URC Plan that I will release next week. Overall, under my presidency, the United States will remain a superpower of the world and will be a safe nation for its citizens.

Before I leave the subject of National Security, let me say that privacy and national security can both be achieved. We are going to repeal the Patriot Act that is one of the most unpatriotic acts passed in the history of our nation. We will not take away basic human rights at the expense of stopping potential terrorists. We will come up with better ways to ensure we are safe. There are two different strategies that could keep us safe: peace through strength, what has kept us pretty much unharmed throughout the last 50 years, or what I call simple peace. Simple peace is the elimination of nuclear weapons and the implementation of more diplomatic ways to tackle situations. I believe a mixture of these are key to safety. The effects of nuclear weapons are bad, and the leaders of countries that have nukes know this. This is why they have only been used twice in human history. Arguments can be made that would say that nukes are good because of this but overall, I would like to eliminate the risk. I would support the destruction of all of our nukes, only if other countries were willing to do the same thing. I would rather avoid a fight but if a fight is to occur, I would like to fight back. I want our military to be so strong we don't have to use it rather than so weak that we can not use it. Ending nuclear capabilities of all counties would be good for humanity as a whole. What is stopping one madman over in North Korea from starting WW3 by pushing the button? When given the choice, I would rather have some damage be caused and some brave soldiers die in warfare than have humans go extinct, but I would rather avoid both scenarios and have us go back to the issues that matter.

Congress has and always will be vastly unpopular. This is because they are unable to properly function due to "party lines". Some things that are more popular than Congress are root canals, lice, traffic jams, and cockroaches * crowd laughs*. I will destroy the party lines and encourage Congress to vote on what is truly good, not what their party leaders say to vote on. I want to work with Congress, no matter who controls the majority, to help America seek something better. That is exactly what we will do ladies and gentlemen: seek something better. We will do this if I am elected President. So, everyone, I have officially begun one hell of a journey that will be spent fighting for all of us. I am running for President of the United States. Thank you- Thank you very much *cheers*

This speech would resonate well with most and would be one of the first times I will be given mainstream media attention. It will work out for me and my campaign.

Chapter Three
Staff And Advisors

"Surround yourself with people who will lift you higher." -Oprah Winfrey

---

It is essential to have good advisors and staff if I am to have a good campaign. I will have 10 great members of my staff that will help America seek something better.

My campaign manager will be someone who has political experience, is scandal free, leans to the right, will not try to run the show, and will be good at raising funds from the people, not special interest groups or super pacs. My campaign manager would be someone like a Rand Paul. My campaign manager would be instructed to raise $500 million solely from the people in the primaries and $1 billion solely from the people in the general election. They also would be instructed to represent me and schedule as many media appearances as possible. Free publicity is the best publicity, whether negative or positive. I would pay my campaign manager a salary of $250,000.

I will also have a chief strategist on my team. I would want them to play mind games with everyone. I would want them to have a step by step plan for everything, say one thing to make someone else say another, etc. They also must be very experienced, but I would prefer them to be an outsider. They could have past experiences in law or in politics in general. I don't care, as long as I trust them and they have a good vision and the determination to go through with that vision, they will be hired. My chief strategist would be someone like an Andrew Jackson or a Trey Gowdy. My chief strategist would get a salary of $200,000 per year.

Thirdly, I will have a political director as a member of the campaign. They will basically be in charge of the campaign decisions and will essentially create the agenda for the campaign. It will be a very important position. This position will be filled by someone who has known me. It will be filled by my past communications director when I got elected to the House of Representatives. The salary for this position will be $175,000.

Also, I will have a communications director on my staff. They will be the main spokesperson of the campaign. They will basically be the ambassador of the Bono campaign. This role will be key to helping us get elected. I would like to simply hire a communications strategist I believe in. I'm not sure who it will be but it will be someone with the mindset of a businessman, possibly a CEO. I like people with a business mindset, they get things done. I want this to be the same for my communications director. Whoever fills this position will get a salary of $150,000.

The fifth position I will have on my staff is social media director. They will need to master something that is key to mastering engagement: social media. If you use it right, you can attract millions of people simply by using 140 characters or posting a picture or phrase. I need help getting engagement up online. I would like every event I have to be live streamed on Facebook and Instagram to attract people to my page. I need an experienced person to help me do this. I would like to hire someone with a social media base themselves that they could bring to me, and then manage. Again, i'm not sure who will fill this position but I would like for it to be someone like Ann Coulter. Whoever fills this position will be paid a $125,000 salary.

The sixth position that will be filled will be my informal advisor. I want my informal advisor to tell me the other side of things. I need him to be what the media might call a "conspiracy theorist". I can tell when things are true or not, I would just like to hear both sides of a story instead of surrounding myself with the same types of people. My informal advisor will basically tell me what he knows or believes in and why. I will then make an opinion on that based on lots of information. I would like this position to be filled by someone like a Matt Drudge or maybe even an Alex Jones. It also very easily could be someone else who fits my criteria. Whoever it ends up being, they will make a salary of $150,000.

The next position that must be filled in my staff is my senior advisor. My senior advisor will be a more trusted source of info so I along with my staff don't get too heavily criticized. It will be someone like a Marco Rubio or a Bernie Sanders. My senior advisor will simply advise me on issues. They will get paid $150,000. The eighth position on my staff will be my policy director. My policy director will do the obvious: help solve policy issues. They will help me out on policy issues. The position will be filled by someone that simply has beliefs that coincide with my own, like a Rand Paul or a Ted Cruz or a Donald Trump. The senior advisor will get a salary of $125,000.

The ninth position in my staff will be my national security/foreign policy advisor. They will advise me on all issues in relation to national security or foreign policy. I would like this person to have military experience but not be a warmonger. We'll see who this person ends up being. They will earn a $175,000 salary.

The final position on my staff will be my delegate strategist. My delegate strategist will help draw paths for me to get the Republican nomination. This will help me know where to campaign. They then will help me in the general election by making paths to 270 electoral votes. I would like this position to be given to someone who has had past election experience. I want this position to be filled by someone like John Kasich. My delegate strategist will receive a salary of $125,000.

Overall, I will have a great staff that will work effortlessly with me to help us seek something better, and they will have key roles in making me the President of the United States in 2040.

Chapter Four
The Media

"Whoever controls the media, controls the mind." -Jim Morrison

_____

The media is essential to winning an election. You need coverage. You need your name to get out there. You need people to see your message. You must manipulate the media.

The first part of my plan involves getting immediate coverage in the beginning of the campaign. I don't care if the coverage is good or bad, as long as I am covered. I want my name to stick in the media for a long time. This will probably be done do to statements I made or will make. I also will invite the media to all of my "big announcements" that will really just be campaign rallies. The rallies will be small at first but media coverage will make them larger.

Step two of my plan is to get the media to interview me. Offer "exclusive" interviews. This will only be done during the first 1-2 months of my campaign. This will once again help my message get to people and it will seem as though I am being transparent. I also will get my message out via ads. Ads will be talked about more in depth later on but my ad campaign will be amazing.

Step three of my media plan is to turn on the media. I will criticize them, as everyone should be criticized. No one in this world is exempt from criticism. The media will then begin to cover me more negatively, and more often, which will benefit me.

Step four is to turn the public against the media, even more than they are right now. According to Gallup, a mere 32% of people trust the mainstream media. That number should be lower, and i'll make sure that it will be. My huge amount of supporters will all be turned against the media because of me. It won't be violent, they simply won't trust or follow the mainstream media. I myself have, to an extent, amounts of respect or trust in the media but it is better for my campaign if the media is manipulated. Also, the small amount of trust I do have in the mainstream media could disappear overnight if they continue to report or act the way that they do. MSNBC for example is a total joke. CNN is bad and biased but still slightly ok, FOX is biased, NBC and ABC just follow CNN, and BBC is probably the best in terms of accurate and fair reporting.

Step five is to expose the media. 6 companies control 90% of the media in America. These 6 companies are General Electric, News-Corp, Disney, Viacom, Time Warner, and CBS. No wonder you are fed the same information from practically every channel you go to. 232 media executives control the information that is given to over 277 million Americans. This is means each media executive controls what about 1.2 million people see. The revenue in 2010 of these 6 companies was about $280 billion. This was $40 billion more than the GDP of Finland, or enough to buy every NFL team 12 times, and still have money leftover. 178 million different users read Time Warner's news each month. The News-Corp company owns the top newspaper in 3 continents. In 2010, News-Corp avoided $1 billion in taxes. This is enough to double the budget of FEMA or to fund NPR 40 times. Box office sales of the 6 companies was $7 billion in 2010. This is double the sales of the next 140 studios combined. It's sad... back in 1983, 90% of the media was controlled by 50 companies. Overall, there are 1,500 magazines, 1,100 newspapers, 9,000 radio stations, 1,500 TV stations, and 2,400 publishers run by these 6 companies. If more people knew this, the approval rating of the mainstream media would surely drop. The media would surely fight this, even though you can't fight facts, and I would get even more coverage.

Step six is to funnel mainstream media viewers over to my social media page. Like I said earlier, every single event I have will be livestreamed and posted onto my social media pages. I also will make lots of announcements on my social media page, forcing people to follow me, including the media, if they would like to hear what I have to say, and they will definitely want to hear what I have to say as at this point I will have formed large group of supporters and will be the favorite to win the nomination. People will watch my speeches on social media rather than the media.

Finally, step seven will be to maintain the position I will be in. I will have won my war with the media and annihilated their credibility. I will have a huge following on social media and anyone who still watches the mainstream media will still watch constant coverage of me.

Chapter Five
Funding

"It always seems impossible until it's done"
-Nelson Mandela

I will spend more than any other candidate in history on my campaign. I will get $500 million by the convention and will get another $1 billion through the general election season. Overall, I will spend $1.5 billion on my campaign. Here's the breakdown of my sources of revenue during the campaign.

PRIMARIES

Type Of Donor	Percentage Of Revenue
Individual	80%
Super Pacs	<1%
RNC	13%
Other	6%

The vast majority of funding will come from individuals and practically no funding will come from super PACs.

GENERAL ELECTION

Type Of Donor	Percentage Of Revenue
Individuals	81%
Super Pacs	1%
RNC	17%
Other	1%

Again, the vast majority of my funding will come from individuals in the general election. 98% of my revenue comes from the RNC and individual donations.

I will spend 100% of what I receive and overall will run a good successful campaign.

Chapter Six
The Primary Rallies

"Government is not the solution to the problem; government is the problem." -Ronald Reagan

---

My first rally will be in May of 2039. It will be in whatever state the first primary will be in. I will have a town hall there later that week as well. I will have basically one political rally per day, sometimes two or three. I will put a possible schedule below with the location and the estimated size of the crowd. I would like to hold a rally with 50,000 people in attendance in each state throughout the primary season.

Possible Schedule
- May 2- State where first primary is, 5,000 in crowd
- May 3- Pennsylvania, Wells Fargo Center, 20,000 in crowd
- May 4- North Carolina, Cameron Indoor Stadium, 9,000 in crowd

- May 5- South Carolina, Bon Secours Wellness Arena, 12,000 in crowd
- May 6- Atlanta, Georgia, Phillips Arena, 20,000 in crowd
- May 7- State where first primary is, first town hall, 7,500 in crowd
- May 8- Utah, Vivint Smart Home Arena, 20,000 in crowd
- May 9- Nevada, T-Mobile Arena, 15,000 in crowd
- May 10- Arizona, Scottsdale Stadium, 10,000 in crowd
- May 11- Michigan, The Palace of Auburn Hills, 20,000 in crowd
- May 12- State where first primary is, 10,000 in crowd
- May 13- Missouri, Scottrade Center, 17,500 in crowd
- May 14- Pennsylvania, Beaver Stadium, 50,000+ in crowd
- June 5- Texas, Globe Life Park, 50,000+ in crowd
- June 10- North Dakota, Alerus Center, 50,000+ in crowd
- June 11- New Hampshire, SNHU Arena, 10,000 in crowd
- June 12- Maine, Alfond Arena, 10,000 in crowd

- June 17- Kentucky, Commonwealth Stadium, 50,000+ in crowd
- June 19- Oregon, Moda Center, 20,000 in crowd
- June 25- Colorado, Broadmoor World Arena, 10,000 in crowd
- July 1- Florida, FIU Stadium, 20,000 in crowd
- July 2- Alaska, Sullivan Arena, 10,000 in crowd
- July 3- Illinois, Toyota Park, 25,000 in crowd
- July 4- Louisiana, Independence Stadium, 50,000+ in crowd
- July 16- Connecticut, Yale Bowl, 50,000+ in crowd
- July 24- Virginia, Bridgeforth Stadium, 25,000 in crowd
- July 30- Ohio, Quicken Loans Arena, 20,000 in crowd
- August 5- Indiana, Memorial Stadium, 50,000+ in crowd
- August 7- Tennessee, Liberty Bowl Memorial Stadium, 50,000+ in crowd
- August 16- West Virginia, WVU Coliseum, 15,000 in crowd
- August 19- Kansas, Allen Fieldhouse, 17,500 in crowd

- August 24- New Mexico, The Pit, 15,000 in crowd
- August 26- Oklahoma, Boone Pickens Stadium, 50,000+ in crowd
- August 27- Iowa, UNI Dome, 17,500 in crowd
- August 28- Idaho, Albertsons Stadium, 50,000+ in crowd
- September 9- Arkansas, War Memorial Stadium, 50,000+ in crowd
- September 11- New York, Yankee Stadium, 50,000+ in crowd
- September 17- Wisconsin, Miller Park, 50,000+ in crowd
- September 24- Minnesota, Mariucci Arena, 10,000 in crowd
- September 30- Florida, Bright House Networks Stadium, 50,000+ in crowd
- October 2-Alabama, Ladd=Peebles Stadium, 50,000+ in crowd
- October 7- Mississippi, M. M. Roberts Stadium, 50,000+ in crowd
- October 8- Hawaii, Aloha Stadium, 50,000+ in crowd
- October 9- Massachussetts, Fitton Field, 25,000 in crowd
- October 12- New Jersey, High Point Solutions Stadium, 50,000+ in crowd

- October 14- Rhode Island, Brown Stadium, 50,000+ in crowd
- October 16- Nebraska, TD Ameritrade Park Omaha, 50,000+ in crowd
- October 18- South Dakota, Dana J. Dykhouse Stadium, 50,000+ in crowd
- October 20- California, Staples Center, 20,000 in crowd
- October 21- California, Angel Stadium of Anaheim, 50,000+ in crowd
- October 23- Washington, Joe Albi Stadium, 25,000 in crowd
- October 25- Oregon, Reser Stadium, 50,000+ in crowd
- October 28- Vermont, Centennial Field, 25,000 in crowd
- October 29- Maryland, Navy Marine Corps Memorial Stadium, 50,000+ in crowd
- October 30- Delaware, Delaware Stadium, 50,000+ in crowd
- November 1- Ewing M. Kauffman Stadium, 50,000+ in crowd
- November 4- Montana, Metrapark Arena, 15,000 in crowd
- November 5- Wyoming, Arena Auditorium, 20,000 in crowd

- November 6- Colorado, Coors Field, 50,000+ in crowd
- November 10- Arizona, Chase Field, 50,000+ in crowd
- November 12- Kansas, University of Kansas Memorial Stadium, 50,000+ in crowd
- November 14- Ohio, InfoCision Stadium, 50,000+ in crowd
- November 15- Montana, Washington-Grizzly Stadium, 50,000+ in crowd
- November 18- Virginia, EagleBank Arena, 15,000 in crowd
- November 19- North Carolina, PNC Arena, 25,000 in crowd
- November 20- Pennsylvania, PNC Park, 30,000 in crowd
- November 25- Texas, Gerald J. Ford Stadium, 50,000+ in crowd
- November 27- South Carolina, Williams-Brice Stadium, 50,000+ in crowd
- November 29- Iowa, Jack Trice Stadium, 50,000+ in crowd
- December 4- state where first primary is, 20,000 in crowd

- December 10- New Mexico, University Stadium, 50,000+ in crowd
- December 11- Georgia, Turner Field, 50,000+ in crowd
- December 16- Massachussetts, Harvard Stadium, 25,000 in crowd
- December 21- Michigan, Waldo Stadium, 30,000 in crowd
- December 30- Alaska, Anchorage Football Field, 25,000 in crowd
- December 31- Pennsylvania, Hershey Park Arena, 10,000 in crowd
- January 1- California, Honda Center, 17,500 in crowd
- January 5- Utah, Rice Eccles Stadium, 50,000+ in crowd
- January 6- Indiana, Banker's Life Fieldhouse, 15,000 in crowd
- January 10- Michigan, Comerica Park, 50,000+ in crowd
- January 13- Minnesota, Target Field, 50,000+ in crowd
- January 15- Maine, Cross Insurance Arena, 10,000 in crowd
- January 20- Nevada, Sam Boyd Stadium, 50,000+ in crowd
- January 22- New Hampshire, Wildcat Stadium, 25,000 in crowd

- January 28- Illinois, Huskie Stadium, 50,000+ in crowd
- February 3- Massachusetts, Fenway Park, 50,000+ in crowd
- February 5- Florida, Lockhart Stadium, 20,000 in crowd
- February 7- Virginia, John C. Edwards Stadium, 50,000+ in crowd
- February 11- Wisconsin, Kohl Center, 20,000 in crowd
- February 17- North Carolina, Ficklen Stadium, 50,000+ in crowd
- February 21- Iowa, Wells Fargo Arena, 15,000 in crowd
- February 25- Oregon, Matthew Knight Arena, 12,500 in crowd
- February 26- New Hampshire, International Speedway, 50,000+ in crowd
- March 2- North Carolina, Cameron Indoor Stadium, 10,000 in crowd
- March 4- New Mexico, Isotopes Park, 15,000 in crowd
- March 7- Oregon, Hayward Field, 12,500 in crowd
- March 11- Florida- Amalie Arena, 15,000 in crowd

- March 17- Wyoming, War Memorial Stadium, 50,000+ in crowd
- March 18- Virginia, John Paul Jones Arena, 15,000 in crowd
- March 21- California, Titian Stadium, 12,500 in crowd
- March 23- Pennsylvania, Howard J. Lamade Stadium, 45,000 in crowd
- March 24- Florida, Blue Wahoos Stadium, 10,000 in crowd
- March 25- Ohio, Nationwide Arena, 12,500 in crowd
- March 30- Michigan, Crisler Center, 12,500 in crowd
- April 5- Iowa, Buccaneer Arena, 5,000 in crowd
- April 6- Arizona, Surprise Stadium, 10,000 in crowd
- April 8- Nevada, Reno EVents Center, 7,500 in crowd
- April 10- New Hampshire, Holman Stadium, 7,500
- April 14- Alaska, The Dome, 50,000+ in crowd
- April 20- Florida, BB&T Center, 12,500 in crowd
- April 22- Colorado, 1stBank Center, 7,500 in crowd

- April 28- Pennsylvania, Giant Center, 10,000 in crowd
- May 3- Florida, American Airlines Arena, 20,000 in crowd
- May 5- New Hampshire, SNHU Arena, 12,500 in crowd
- May 9- Minnesota, Williams Arena, 12,500 in crowd
- May 11- Wisconsin, BMO Harris Bradley Center, 15,000 in crowd
- May 12- Ohio, Huntington Center, 7,500 in crowd
- May 13- Arizona, University Of Phoenix Stadium, 25,000 in crowd
- May 14- New Mexico, Roswell Convention Center, 2,500 in crowd
- May 16- California, Redding Civic Auditorium, 2,500 in crowd
- May 17- Oregon, Providence Park, 15,000 in crowd
- May 19- Connecticut, XL Center, 15,000 in crowd
- May 22- New Jersey, Red Bull Arena, 20,000 in crowd
- May 25- Maine, Alfond Stadium, 50,000+ in crowd
- May 26- Rhode Island, Dunkin Donuts Center, 10,000 in crowd

- May 31- Pennsylvania, Beaver Stadium, 75,000+ in crowd

Chapter Seven
The First Debate

"Without debate, without criticism, no administration and no country can succeed-- and no republic can survive." -John F. Kennedy

---

The first Republican debate should be sometime between May and August of 2039. Going into the debate, I intend to be in the top 3 in terms of polling. The debate will be a great opportunity for me to get my name and policies out there without having to pay a premium for ads. There will also be far more viewers of the debate than almost any ad could attract. I will spend about 70% of my speaking time talking about my policies and 30% of my speaking time attacking other candidates and their policies or history. My attacks will be very effective. I am going to get as much attention as is possible during this debate.

Overall, the first debate will be a very good experience and will help my numbers spike. My crowd sizes will grow after the first debate and step three of my media plan will commence at my first rally after the debate after I get good coverage and reviews from the media.

Chapter Eight
The First
Primary/Caucus

"There's no such thing as a free lunch."
-Milton Friedman

I probably will lose the first primary or caucus. I was a one term governor of Pennsylvania and member of the House of Representatives. I wasn't even a Senator. This however doesn't mean that I won't win the nomination or won't get any delegates from the first primary or caucus.

I expect there to be 10 candidates in the race at this point. I then expect to place in third in the first primary with about 24% of the vote. I will get some delegates for this as well. Following defeat in the first primary, with nothing else to lose, I will have delegates to gain. I will drastically improve my ground game and will have my delegate strategist give me five separate scenarios in which I win certain states that will win me the nomination. I will then go through with the plans and win far more delegates and eventually the nomination.

Chapter Nine
Future
Primaries/Caucuses

"To be prepared for war is one of the most effectual means of preserving peace."

After my defeat in the first primary or caucus, I will win every single primary or caucus after that until "Super Tuesday" comes. I will win the majority of the states on "Super Tuesday" and will have very good leads in the delegate race.

I then will continue to run a great ad campaign, ground game, and overall campaign and will win many more primaries and caucuses until eventually clinching the Republican nomination sometime between April and May.

Chapter Ten
Future Debates And
Quorums

"An investment in knowledge pays the best interest." -Benjamin Franklin

---

After having a fairly good performance in the first debate, I will go into future debates with a little bit of momentum. I will stay steady in the top 3 in polling until the first primary or caucus. My numbers will go down a little bit but I will still be in third after I lose in the first primary or caucus. After the second primary or caucus, I will move up to second and come the fourth primary or caucus, I will narrowly be in first. I then will hold this momentum into "Super Tuesday" attacking my challenger in all ways I can on the debate stage.

I will widen the gap more and more by running more and more adds and doing more and more good performances in debates and quorums and will eventually clinch the nomination. I will be in the public eye during almost all of the debates and the battle for the nomination will be ruthless, but I will prevail.

Chapter Eleven
Getting The Nomination

"It's a damn poor mind indeed which can't think of at least two ways to spell any word."

-Andrew Jackson

It will take a lot of effort to win the nomination, but I will do it. Countless rallies will need to be held in key states, but you must do more than hold a rally. You must engage with the voters if you are to win.

As I said before, I believe I will lose the first primary or caucus. I believe I will get about 23% of the vote in the primary or caucus and will get some delegates. I'm going to totally make up a schedule that has been similar in previous years to base what I am about to say from. No matter what the schedule is, I will get the nomination. This schedule is just a hypothetical situation with results I believe I will be able to achieve, but we'll see in 2040.

Schedule

Date, State Caucus/Primary, Delegates Available, Delegates I Will Win

February 1, Iowa Caucus, 33, 8

February 7, New Hampshire Primary, 18, 6

February 18, South Carolina Primary, 33, 33

February 28, Nevada Caucus, 30, 12

March 6, Alaska Caucus, 28, 9

March 6, Arkansas Primary, 37, 13

March 6, Georgia Primary, 75, 26

March 6. Massachusetts Primary, 42, 13

March 6, Minnesota Caucus, 36, 10

March 6, Oklahoma Primary, 41, 11

March 6, Tennessee Primary, 56, 24

March 6, Vermont Primary, 17, 7

March 6, Virginia Primary, 49, 16

March 10, Kansas Caucus, 41, 15

March 10, Louisiana Primary, 45, 20

March 13, Alabama Primary, 48, 21

March 13, Hawaii Caucus, 20, 9

March 13, Mississippi Primary, 40, 19

March 20, Florida Primary, 70, 70

March 20, Illinois Primary, 67, 27

March 20, Missouri Primary, 54, 25

March 20, North Carolina Primary, 62, 30

March 27, Arizona Primary, 44, 44

March 27, Ohio Primary, 65, 40

March 27, Utah Caucus, 40, 40

April 10, Wisconsin Primary, 41, 14
April 10, Michigan Primary, 45, 29
April 10, Maryland Primary, 37, 37
April 10, Texas Primary, 150, 85
April 14, Colorado Convention, 30, 0
April 24, New York Primary, 95, 75
April 24, Connecticut Primary, 28, 20
April 24, Delaware Primary, 16, 13
April 24, Pennsylvania Primary, 45, 45
April 24, Rhode Island Primary, 18, 7
May 1, Indiana Primary, 52, 52
May 1, West Virginia, 31, 20
May 8, Oregon Primary, 26, 12
May 8, Nebraska Caucus, 35, 25
May 15, Washington Primary, 42, 26
May 22, California Primary, 172, 125
May 22, Montana Caucus, 26, 19
May 22, New Jersey Primary, 50, 50
May 22, New Mexico Primary, 25, 19
May 22, South Dakota Primary 27, 23
May 22, Wyoming Caucus, 29, 24
May 22, Idaho Caucus, 33, 27
May 22, North Dakota Caucus, 28, 25

Chapter Twelve
The Convention

"As it is an ancient truth that freedom cannot be legislated into existence, so it is no less obvious that freedom can not be censored into existence" -Dwight D. Eisenhower

---

The 2040 Republican National Convention should be held at The Palace of Auburn Hills in Auburn Hills, Michigan. I will be officially nominated there at some point between July and August of 2040. The convention will last four days, as usual, and there will be many guest speakers. It will be a great opportunity to showcase what the party has to offer that year.

I will give a speech at the convention on the last day of the convention. Below is the likely transcript of that speech.

"Thank you, thank you. Everyone here tonight watching and in the crowd, I have one thing to say: I accept your nomination for President of the United States! *crowd cheers*

I have all of you to thank for this great honor.

It took a great fight to get here, but I am willing to fight for the rest of my days for this country and you the people. I have been fighting for the people since 2022, and I would gladly do it again if I was given the opportunity.

Tonight I am asking all of you, even those who didn't vote for me, to stand in solidarity with our great movement. This is not a political party issue. This is a common sense issue. We have many problems that we are facing, and my opponent absolutely can not solve them. They have no chance. Zero. I am also asking you to join us on the journey to prosperity.

Under my administration, we will be a nation of prosperity where you the people matter and we the people take back control of our government. For far too long have the Washington insiders run the game, and that game was established to be against you. We must unite against this. I vow to every

American tonight that I will fight against the elite who control our government.

Last night you heard a speech from my Vice Presidential pick. I think he is a fantastic person and will work side by side with us to help us seek something better.

We will seek something better in education. We are ranked 14th worldwide in education. When is it ever acceptable to come in 14th place? We as a country are the greatest in the world, our leaders however are not. They are to blame for our horrible rankings in education. We will fix this with a few steps.

Step one is to change the outdated schedule. The whole system is outdated. We're going to change the system requirements, and let local government decide the rest. Education works best when run locally. We will implement a 4-3 system where students must go to school for four days then get three days off. We're also going to raise the mandatory amount of days you must go to school each year to 210 from 180.

Step two is to is to reform the amount of classes you must take. We will eliminate the 12th grade and replace it with mandatory preschool nationwide. Studies find that if children don't receive early brain stimulation, they will not excel educationally in the future. This is why it will be mandatory to go to preschool in the USA.

Finally, step three is to end property tax based education. Lots of states rely on property taxes to fund education but since wealthy houses are worth more, they pay more in property taxes. This means that the wealthy zip codes get better schools and typically a better education than the rest of America. It will vary by states and be up to the states to determine the amount, but the amount of money that funds public education will need to be flat. If California collects $100 million and has 100 zip codes, each zip code gets $1 million in funding. Too long have the elite benefited from the rest of us. No longer will this happen, especially in our educational system. Overall, the educational system in America under my administration will thrive, and will certainly be better than it is right now.

We will seek something better in our tax system. For years, the tax system has been disproportionate. Even the solutions to our current tax system are disproportionate. This is why we will have a 20% flat tax rate. We will also make sure the elite do not exploit our tax system by eliminating all deductions and loopholes currently available and currently used by many. Every four years we will also have a total tax vacation in which no one pays any federal income tax. It will be amazing for all of us and the economy.

We will seek something better in the Federal Reserve. I did not release my plan for the Federal Reserve yet, and what better time is there to do so? We are going to End the monopoly of banks known as the Federal Reserve. The Federal Reserve, created in 1913, has caused the value of the dollar to lose a little over 95% of it's value. In 1913, for $4.10, you could buy $100 worth of stuff. The reason the money is worth less is because the more money there is in existence, the less each bill is worth.

The Federal Reserve is a debt machine. The Federal Reserve is responsible for over $2.5

trillion of our National Debt. The way the system works is that whenever the government wants money, the issue treasury bonds. These treasury bonds are then sold to the Federal Reserve in exchange for "Federal Reserve Notes", or dollars. These dollars were created out of thin air and have no value whatsoever. You see, they used to have value. You used to be able to turn in you ten dollar bill for ten dollars worth of gold. Those slips of paper had actual value. Now, what's a piece of paper worth?

Anyways, the U.S. must pay interest on the money they borrowed from the Fed, the only problem is this: If you borrowed the first dollar into existence but promised to pay it back, plus interest, how do you pay it back? You can't! You must continuously borrow.

The whole system is a scam and the banks make billions in profits each year from it. We will lend it entirely. It will be replaced with a system much much better, one where actual things of value are used as currency. Both gold and silver will be used as currency in the U.S. The U.S. Treasury will print our money now, so no National Debt is added while printing and the process is interest free. The money can be redeemed by all for either the value in gold or silver. The gold or silver can also be redeemed at any time for it's value in dollars, and so on. We will print a limited amount of dollars each year due to the fact they must be backed by a limited amount of gold and silver. This will stop us from mass producing dollars at the expense of devaluing our currency and creating debt. There is a problem, and it will be solved.

America will always solve the problems it is facing. No longer will we allow problems to build up and become bigger ones, or even develop in the first place. Patient diplomacy is a synonym for doing nothing.

We will seek something better in foreign policy. We will be anti-interventionist 100%. 100%. With my opponent, you would get involved in many useless wars. We will lead America back to prosperity rather than Iraq back to poverty at the cost of $2.4 trillion and thousands of lives. If another country is in a civil war, we will let them sort out their problems. The only time we as a nation will get involved is if we are threatened, both verbally and literally. We do not tolerate disrespect of our great nation.

Patriotism will rise once again under my administration.

We will also cut foreign aid in half and will cut troop levels worldwide in half. They will train here in the U.S. until they are needed. This doesn't mean that we will not improve our military. We will have a military so strong that we don't have to use it rather than one so weak that we can't use it. I will increase military spending and get much more out of the spending than we currently do.

We will seek something better in immigration. Illegal immigration is a problem, and we must solve it. Each year, at the state local and federal level, illegal immigration costs taxpayers about $113 billion. In no other country in the world can you break the country's laws and be rewarded.

Most illegals don't pay taxes. Some do, most don't. Less than 50% of illegals pay taxes. Most the money they pay into taxes, about $12 billion, they get back. In addition, the amount they pay in taxes is just about 10% of their cost. They certainly aren't paying for everything they get.

Illegals who don't pay taxes will be deported, effective immediately. Illegals in our prisons will be deported as well. Illegals who pay taxes and have no criminal record will be given a choice: be escorted out of the country and come back in legally and get full citizenship or immediately get permanent residency. With permanent residency, you are not given the right to vote. You lose the right to vote when you come here illegally. If they decide to leave and come back, they will get the right to vote as they will become citizens.

We will change the laws regarding legal immigration to this country as well. The U.S. will cap the amount of people it accepts into the U.S. each year at 0.15% of the U.S. population at the last census. Those who decide to leave the country and come back in legally will not be counted on this tally. We will also change the amount of time you can stay on the waiting list without reply to one year. Within one year of your filing for citizenship, you will get a response. Finally, we will implement a queue system in which those who can contribute more get accepted first. No longer will it be first come first serve. If there was someone with a college education applying for citizenship and someone without one applying, the one with a college education will get accepted first.

Now, back to illegal immigration. Here are some statistics for everyone. In 2014, about 50% of federal crimes were committed near the U.S. Mexico border. Also, in 2014, illegals accounted for about 75% of federal drug sentences. About 50% of illegals came from Mexico. This is why we will secure the Mexico-U.S. border with enhanced new security. The cost of this new security will be about $11.3 billion per year. This is in addition to the current amount spent. This $11.3 billion is 10% of the amount illegals cost us each year. Also, since the $11.3 billion prevents illegal immigration, it saves money. I'm not done with the statistics. About 8% of the illegal population is in prison as opposed to about 0.8% of the legal population. There are a mere 1,000 illegal Americans in Mexico as opposed to about 6 million illegal Mexicans in the U.S. and believe me, you don't get the same benefits as an illegal in Mexico. Illegals account for 5%-30% of convictions for murder and rape despite representing a mere 3.5% of the U.S. population.

If we removed every single illegal immigrant by deportation it would cost about $500 billion. It takes less than 5 years for the U.S. to spend this amount of money on illegals. I won't do this though because some of them are good people. Some are criminal tax evaders but some actually are good.

Overall, illegal immigration in my administration will be a thing of the past. We will begin the deportation of the bad illegals on my first day in office and will begin the process of permanent residency or citizenship on the first day as well. Legals will be able to come to the U.S. legally and the best will get to enter the best country in the world first!

Finally, we will seek something better in Social Security. Social Security is a system that accounts for $2.8 trillion of debt. This is about 14% of our national debt. This money is owed to the trust fund by the U.S. Treasury, but in order for the treasury to get money, they must create more debt.

You might be wondering why this money is owed. Well, the answer is that the government wasted it, or stole from we the people. The money was spent on wars and other government programs. Your stolen money was wasted.

Social Security takes 6.2% out of your paycheck each year and in return, on average, gives you about $16,000 each year. This is a mere $4,300 above the poverty line, and that poverty line is for single people. If married, that poverty line is $16,000, or the average benefit received.

According to Gallup, 33.3% of Americans have no retirement savings and therefore will be forced to live slightly above or at the poverty line. This however is right now. By 2034, benefits are estimated to be cut 23%. This means the average annual benefit will reach $12,300. Now, if you are single, you are $500 over the poverty level and if you are married, you are $3,700 below the poverty level, and this is just 17 years from now. Imagine what our current 18 year olds will get when they retire.

Don't worry, I have a solution to this devastating problem. If we made it law that employers must put 3.7% of your annual salary into a retirement savings account, and assumed you made the average salary in America of about $45,000, you would make $3,375 a month for retirement instead, at about ⅓ of the cost. The best part is it is no cost to you the people, the cost in solely on the employer's and believe me, this is no burden to them. They make astronomical profits, and that's ok, but this won't put them out of business. This system will be implemented whenever the last American who has put money into Social Security dies. This new program won't be able to be implemented until years from now, but it will be a great change for the country and the system as a whole. I also swear to all seniors that I will attempt to increase your monthly pensions.

Political divisiveness has ruined our country. Lots of people simply listen and obey to what their party leaders say they should do, especially those on the other side. They ignore the facts or call them or yourself key phrases like "racist", "fascist", or "conspiracy theorists". Some of these people will defend their party or their leaders no matter what they do. It's horrible. I am reaching beyond all of the party lines and trying to get every American's vote. I am not tied to the Republicans or the Democrats, I am tied to you the people.

I will restore an era of victory and prosperity into our nation. We are going to eliminate the entire national debt within eight years if we are given the chance to. The only way for this to happen is for all of you to go out and vote on November 6th!

The American dream has been destroyed by Washington. Washington has regulated and taxed the incentives out of all of us. Companies put their jobs over in China, fire their employees, and expect no consequences. Americans for years have been wanting to seek something better, but there was nothing in sight. I have laid out plans that will bring back the American dream and will restore the legacy of greatness in America, a legacy that has been absent for decades.

We deserve better, and I will give you better. America has been mocked by the world for years. America has been full of poverty. For years America has been defeated. It is time to bring America back to victory, and bring our people along with us.

In our America, the America in which we the people are in charge and our country is a free and safe nation with free and safe markets, we are the superpower of the world. Right now we are not. If we would like the heart of our nation that beats the blood of patriots to be restored, then you must go out ad vote, go out and volunteer, go out and help our movement be a successful one and help us seek something better! Our country will be made so much better with your help. We the people will seek something better and restore prosperity in America! Thank you, thank you all, god bless you and god bless the USA!

Chapter Thirteen
The General Election Rallies

"Whenever you do a thing, act as if all the world were watching." -Thomas Jefferson

My general election rallies will be amazing. They will attract thousands of people each time. I will hold about 2 rallies per day between July and September and then in the months of October and November, I will hold about 4 rallies per day. Locations of the rallies will vary by polling but I will hold rallies in all 50 states, as I did in the primaries, and my goal this time will be to attract 75,000 people at at least one rally in each state, even though in some states I should be able to attract over 100,000 supporters.

Overall, these rallies will help me get elected and engage with and attract voters. These rallies will be very energetic and patriotic. At this point, I will have people from across the political spectrum joining our movement and attending the amazing rallies that will help us seek something better!

Chapter Fourteen
The Presidential Debates

"I believe that banking institutions are more dangerous to our liberties than standing armies. If the American people ever allow private banks to control the issue of their currency, first by inflation, then by deflation, the banks and corporations that will grow up around the banks will deprive the people of all property until their children wake-up homeless on the continent their fathers conquered."
-Thomas Jefferson

The three presidential debates should take place in October of 2040. These debates will be used by me to totally derail my opponent's campaign. My rallies will be when I speak of policies and the debates will be spent explaining why my opponent's policies are bad and why mine are better. I will not have any sort of slip up in these debates and will go in with a very good record. I will also try my best to get supporters of mine in the audience and for people to view the debates on my social media pages. Overall, these debates will help my campaign by hurting my opponent's indefinitely. All opposition will be defeated.

Chapter Fifteen
The Ad Campaign

"Everyone wants to live at the expense of the state. They forget that the state wants to live at the expense of everyone." -Frederic Bastiat

---

My ad campaign will be essential to my election. Initially, prior to the primaries, my ads will just speak about me, my views, and information on the campaign.

Getting closer to the primaries, I will begin on of the greatest stream of attack ads America has ever seen. Throughout the primaries my ads will vary but again, due to massive amounts of funds, they will air all day every day and will be very effective.

The same goes for during the general election. During this, I will instruct my communications director to create a new ad every day. I will pay for this and airtime for four hours each day of these ads, always between 5PM and 8PM.

These ads will vary by state but I would say around four ads a week will be attack ads and three ads per week will be ads supporting myself, my ideas, and our movement.

Chapter Sixteen
Election Day

"Liberty cannot be preserved without general knowledge among the people." -John Adams

---

November 6th, 2040 is election day. People across America will go out and vote, and hopefully it will be for me. There should be about 155 million people who vote that election, according to census data and turnout rates. I believe I could get anywhere from 50%-60% of these votes. I also believe I could hit about 330 electoral votes.

Assuming I am victorious, my victory speech will occur at the Wells Fargo Center in Pennsylvania, but either way I will appear here on election night.

Chapter Seventeen
Victory Speech

"Those who stand for nothing fall for anything."
-Alexander Hamilton

Assuming that I win the election on November 6th, 2040, here is a likely transcript of my victory speech.

"Thank you, thank you.

Our opponent has conceded, we are victorious.

Tonight is a historic night in the face of the United States and the world. It also is a historic night for those who are attempting to rule over us like dictators as they will never gain access to our great country again. We have defeated the monopoly they have, and we will destroy that very monopoly.

Our country will solve the problems we are facing, and we are facing many problems, but we will do so as a country, not just as myself or Congress or any single individual. You voted me into this position to lead so now I will lead in this position for you the people.

I vow to every American tonight that I will fight for and alongside you.

Whether you voted for me or not, I will represent you. I will represent the United States of America as a whole. I will restore the legacy of prosperity into America the likes of which has not been seen since Andrew Jackson, 2 centuries ago.

We the people have just taken back control of the government. This hard fought battle was fought not to elect me but to fix our great country to restore the American dream, to bring money and jobs back, to fix the tax system, to fix our whole country, together as one nation, under god.

I will destroy party lines, and I will do it for we the people. For too long has our country been divided. Whether it was the North and the South, the federalists or the anti-federalists, or the Republicans or the Democrats, they all divided our country. They forced us to not live or believe by choice but rather believe in what party leaders tell us to believe in. You know you are doing something good when the elite don't like or support you. We have been challenged by the elite because they know we are going to end their monopoly and give the power to all Americans. With that being said, I don't care if you have lots of money, that doesn't ,matter. I don't care if you are greedy, that is essential. What I care about, and you should to, is the fact that some of these elitists control, literally control, the gears of our government.

We're pro capitalism, capitalism is an unequal amount of wealth while socialism and communism are equal amounts of poverty. No socialist country has succeeded in any way better than capitalist nations. Socialism always fails in the end. Capitalism has it's small amount of flaws but no system is perfect, and capitalism is the greatest economic system to ever be developed throughout the history of the world.

We the country will work together to seek something better. We will do so all over the country. I can tell you one thing, as a matter of fact I will promise this: by the end of my first term, your life will be better than it is right now. I also pledge I won't spend my first term trying to get elected a second, although I believe I will get elected a second term and doing so would allow me to finalize on my policies that are the best, like ending the national debt.

Traveling around the country, our movement drew hundreds, thousands, tens of thousands, and even at points over 100,000 people. Turnout for voting was much higher than this. During this experience, i've gotten to know what all of you must go through and what you all believe in and want. I have formed the largest bond in my life with this country and it's people. This bond is so great as I believe in and love this country. I love this country not because it's perfect, it surely isn't. I love this country because everyone has the potential to be what they are willing to work for. These opportunities aren't just given to the people in terms of jobs, they are given to us in the form of new political figures with new policies.

Our policies will drastically improve our ways of life and our country as a whole, and remember, never forget this: we will seek something better. Thank you everyone, thank you all, god bless you and the United States."

Chapter Eighteen
The Background

"We have a system that increasingly taxes
work and subsidizes nonwork."
-Milton Friedman

I should get elected as governor of
Pennsylvania in 2034. If I am to get elected to
this position, I will need to have a solid
background. Prior to this, I will have been a
member of the House of Representatives in
Pennsylvania's 10th congressional district for 2
terms, mayor of Williamsport, Pennsylvania, a
city council member in Williamsport,
Pennsylvania, and I will have graduated from
Penn State with a degree in political science.

Overall, Pennsylvania will be my new home
state, the people there will love me, and I will
have a great record of being a public servant in
the past so that I can get elected in 2034 for
Governor of Pennsylvania.

Chapter Nineteen
The Announcement

"Live as if you were to die tomorrow. Learn as if you were to live forever." -Mahatma Gandhi

---

My announcement speech will be held on May 1st, 2033. It could be held in many different places but the most likely place in which it will be held is at Howard J Lamade Stadium in Williamsport, Pennsylvania. The announcement speech should get about 3,500 to attend. The speech will be about 2,500 words and will take about 45 minutes to give. Below is a likely transcript of that very speech.

"Thank you all, thank you very much. Let me start off by saying thank you to all of Williamsport who made it possible for me to be here today. Words cannot express how thankful I am for you guys.

Let me also state that today is the beginning of a great journey. I am running for governor of Pennsylvania!

Our great state of Pennsylvania is being overrun and overruled by people that honestly dont give a damn about you. They don't. I however do.

Our leaders in Pennsylvania have created a $130 billion debt. Do you have any idea how much money this is? It would take our city of Williamsport 240 years to earn that much money. 240 years. It is insane.

I will decrease the deficit in Pennsylvania by the end of my first term and will create a surplus each year on our budget.

On the subject of money, let's look at our state's economy. I like the way we are taxed, it's a flat tax. I however don't like the amount. I cut our tax rate from 3.07% to 2.5%. This is about 20% reduction in the rate. Our corporate income tax rates are also extremely high, the second highest in the U.S. to be exact. We will change this to the second lowest in the U.S. We will cut the corporate tax rate to 5% from

10%. If we don't, our people will continuously be unemployed as they have been for years and companies will abandon us. We don't want that do we? We are in the bottom 30% of states in terms of employment rates. 70% of states have a lower unemployment rate than us. In 4 out of the 5 states with the lowest unemployment rates, the corporate tax rate is less than 5%. By the end of my first term, Pennsylvania's unemployment rate will be less than what the U.S. unemployment rate is.

I will also encourage employment by offering a 0.1% tax deduction per 2,000 employees. We will also offer new businesses a tax free first year. This will encourage the development of small businesses and help them grow. New companies that come here to the state of Pennsylvania will also get benefits. Every new plant with 1,000 or more workers built in my administration will receive a 1% tax deduction. Our state will no longer tax businesses out of business. Instead, we will support business and the employment of workers, and overall our economic situation as a whole will be much better off than it is right now.

Crime is actually at OK levels in our state. We have the 23rd highest level. I'd like this to go down to 26th, so that way the majority of states have higher crime rates than us, and that really is the only goal I have for crime rates in our state. If something isn't broken, why would we try to fix it?

Don't let these crime numbers fool you. This is about the only good thing that has come from our leaders, and even the crime levels aren't that astonishing. Most states have lower crime rates. Our government is very inefficient and absolutely does not represent you, as it should. Most voters in our state are registered as Democrats, but that means nothing to me. I have always ran as a Republican but I have never been one. Unfortunately, you can not run as a n indepent successfully or a Libertarian successfully and therefore I choose the Republican party. Yes, I have Republican beliefs but I also have independent beliefs, Libertarian beliefs, and at times Democratic beliefs. I will reach beyond party lines, as I don't identify with any political party, and will do what is best for the people and the state of Pennsylvania, not what is best for the special interest groups.

For too long have Pennsylvanians dealt with crumbling roads, bridges, airports, highways, dams, and overall infrastructure. Act 89 was a step in the right direction but absolutely wasn't enough. 25% of our bridges are structurally deficient, 25% of our dams have high hazard potential, water spread outbreaks are on the rise. While we're on water, let me talk about water fluoridation real quick. Water fluoridation is the only drug forced on the medication with no dosage control. Dozens and dozens of studies have linked water fluoridation to brain damage, and we will repeal the law that makes it illegal to remove fluoridation from our water supply. Ok, now back to infrastructure. Our inland waterways are 150 years old. When they were built, we were fighting in the civil war. They are so old. Our roads are just crumbling and the whole situation is a mess. I will fix it as much as I can in ten years by putting forward $5 billion each year to infrastructure spending. I believe with this large sum of money, I along with other members of government can fix the huge problem regarding infrastructure. If you are to remember one policy from my speech, remember this: I will not add one penny to the state debt.

Immigration will also be enforced in Pennsylvania. Federal laws have made it clear that we must obey their laws in regards to immigration. We have 18 sanctuary cities in Pennsylvania. This is the same amount they have in California. This is absurd! We will end all sanctuary cities in our state and let the federal government remove who they believe they should remove, but we will not aid criminals/foreigners, that is the definition of treason. In about half of the states in the U.S., there are no sanctuary cities. We will become one of those states as well in 2034!

Education in Pennsylvania is OK in the K-12 level. We are 12th in the U.S. in K-12. We however our the worst state in the country for higher education the worst. Pennsylvania should never be last in anything, ever. Yet here we are. We will fix the schedule in Pennsylvania for K-12 education as well as the funding for higher education. We drastically fund K-12 education in preparation for college but hardly do anything for college. You can prepare as much as you want for a battle but you still have no control of that battle. This is how it is right now in terms of education.

The K-12 schedule will be changed so that we have a 4-3 system. Four days of school and then 3 days off. This system will go on for however many days local governments want, as long as students attend school for at least 200 days each year.

In terms of higher education, we will drastically increase the budget. We will raise the budget for higher education to $750 million from $450 million. Now, with that being said, simply giving more money to the system doesn't help. Throwing money at a trashcan doesn't make it perform any better. I am not an educator and I have nothing to do with that area, so I will appoint and instruct a great individual to lead the Department of Education back to prosperity, as well as higher education. Education will be great in my administration and failed education will be a thing of the past.

I'm not sure if I've said it enough yet, so I'll say it again: I will not add a penny to the state debt. Not one cent, and as a matter of fact, I will create a surplus each year. I will lower the income tax rate to 2.5% flat. I will end the death and estate tax, end the tire fee, raise cigarette tax to $5 per pack from $2.6, raise liquor tax from 18% to 20%, cut corporate tax rate from 10% to 5%, cut vehicle lease and rent taxes in half, and cut sales tax from 6% to 5%. The total revenue from all of this will be about $35 billion. Pennsylvania will spend approximately $34.99 billion each year, generating a surplus on the budget that will be put towards a rainy day fund. I, unlike most other governors, will help end the state debt. My opponents will just increase it even more and then eventually stick you with the bill. Horrible.

Socially, I am pretty center, and overall I am a libertarian. I believe the second amendment shouldn't tampered with even more than it is right now, and I believe concealed carry of handguns should be legalized statewide without a need for permits. The second amendment is your permit, and it never expires! States like Alaska and Vermont allow this, and they have one of the lowest gun crime rates.

On abortion, I believe it should be avoided at all costs, but I will obey the Supreme Court and allow it to be the women's choice, but this choice will have limitations. I do not have the right to kill a human with fully developed organs and tissues, a heartbeat, brain waves, and feelings, and neither should anyone else. Babies can feel pain at 10 weeks, have fully functioning organs at 8 weeks, have brain waves measured at about 8 weeks, and develop a heartbeat at week 3. For this reason, we will ban abortion after 12 weeks, or 3 months. Right now, in our state, abortion is banned after 6 months, but at this point a baby is already yawing, feeling pain, and has a consciousness. A consciousness! It feels the knife going into the back of it's neck and knows it is dying! It's sick! Again, I'm fine with you getting an abortion, the law of the land is that it's legal. Murder is however illegal, and killing a conscious being with brainwaves, a heartbeat, and fully functioning organs is murder.

On free speech, I, along with almost everyone, am a strong advocate for it. I don't believe any of our taxpayer dollars should be spent on censoring free speech or regulate how we communicate via social media, or in any way. Our state representatives have been passing anti free speech legislation for years now. It's insanity! Under my administration, we will spend none of your money on censorship or regulation of your constitutional rights.

Electing me will be a total takeover of our government! We the people will have total control of the government. No longer will the incentives be taxed out of us, will we censor free speech, will we allow murder of babies, will we add money to the state debt, will we advocate for gun control, which is the very reason we have gun related deaths, will we have schools that rank in last, and no longer will we discourage patriotism.

We the people will take back our government in a revolution unlike anything they have ever seen before! We the people of Pennsylvania will end the lies, thank you, god bless you all, thank you very much!"

Chapter Twenty
The Primary

"Loyalty to country always. Loyalty to government, when it deserves it." -Mark Twain

---

I will run for governor of Pennsylvania in 2034. I believe I will have one or two challengers on the Republican side but that is it. The primary will occur sometime in May of 2034. I believe I will get around 50% of the vote in the primary. This will be more than any other candidate running for governor as a Republican. I will win the primary and will therefore go on to the general election in which I will face my opponent(s).

Chapter Twenty One
The Ad Campaign

""A paranoid is someone who knows a little of what's going on. " -William Burroughs

---

Ads are the key to victory, especially when you are a very unknown one term governor, one term member of city council, and two term member of the house. I will release a new ad every other day in every county in Pennsylvania that will air at primetime on local channels. This will attract the necessary amounts of voters needed to get the nomination and become governor. About 75% of these ads will be attack ads. If you obliterate the other candidate and their reputation, voters only have one other choice: you. Of course, I will also have positive ads about myself. I will have a member of my staff known as the ad director who will help determine what should be in these ads, who to target, when to air the ads, and so on. My ad campaign will be very good, very successful, and very essential to winning the race in 2034.

Chapter Twenty Two
Election Day

"I predict future happiness for Americans, if they can prevent the government from wasting the labors of the people under the pretense of taking care of them." -Thomas Jefferson

---

On November 7, 2034, Pennsylvanians will be able to choose the fate of their great state. They could choose a path of prosperity or a path of continuation and a path of failure. I will have an event planned that night in which I will deliver a speech, and this speech should be a victory speech.

Going into election day, I will have bombarded voters with advertisements and will have a fairly large lead in the polls. I will become the next governor of Pennsylvania in 2034 and will deliver a victory speech on the night of November 7 as voters join me in celebration of our successful movement.

Chapter Twenty Three
Victory Speech

"The heaviest penalty for declining to rule is to be ruled by someone inferior to yourself."
-Plato

On November 7, 2034, I will have officially been elected by the people as governor of Pennsylvania. That night, I will deliver a victory speech from the Hersheypark Arena in Hershey, Pennsylvania. Below is a likely transcript of that speech.

"Wow, thank you. Thank you.

Well, it's official: we won. With less funds and less recognition, we have defeated the establishment. You are the reason we won. Countless amounts of you volunteered and helped me get elected and even more of you went out and voted, and I thank you for that.

Today is the beginning of a new era in Pennsylvania. This era will no longer allow the unemployment rate to be higher than the federal unemployment rate. We will no longer tax the incentives out of both individuals and companies. We will no longer be ranked last in anything, especially education. We will lower the state debt. We will no longer allow our infrastructure to crumble and will no longer fund useless projects that we get hardly nothing out of.

You the people voted to end the lies, and that is exactly what we will do. We have been lied to all of our lives by the establishment. We have been lied to and fooled by them for far too long. Promises have been made but those promises have not been kept. We are different. I saw what was happening to our great state and I realized that I had to do something about it and fix it. Fixing something requires big moves, and I am willing to make those moves, unlike others. These moves will always be in the best interest of our state, not in the best interest of the special interest groups.

Because of you the people, our system is going to be fixed. I will lead our state to prosperity and I will bring you along with me, but I couldn't do anything without you all.

Remember, you are given 100% of the credit for our great and now successful movement. This movement is devoted to ending the failed policies that have ruined our state. We took the initiative to fix our state, and believe me, we will fix it. We will fix it for all of us.

Ever since our state was founded, it was time to end the lies. Today marks the beginning of that process. Thank you all, god bless you, thank you!"

Chapter Twenty Four
Get Politically Involved

"Freedom is never more than one generation away from extinction. We didn't pass it to our children in the bloodstream. It must be fought for, protected, and handed on for them to do the same, or one day we will spend our sunset years telling our children and our children's children what it was once like in the United States where men were free."

You yourself don't have to run for elected office to be politically involved. All you have to do is vote, but it is much better if you volunteer for candidates that align with your views.

Whether you are a Republican, Democrat, Libertarian, Independent, or whatever, you must use your vote to let your voice be heard.

If you do not vote, you lose your voice and should not complain about political issues due to the fact you didn't vote to change it. Even if your candidate loses, you still will have used your voice.

Also, never ever think that you shouldn't vote for a candidate because it seems like the candidate will lose. Wouldn't you rather vote for someone who you think is right and lose than vote for someone who you don't like and then have them win?

You would be surprised at how many people are not politically involved or even politically informed. Here is some information gathered from various polls:

- 36% of Americans can't name all three branches of government, and 35% of them couldn't name any of them. (Business Insider)
- 61% of Americans don't know what political party controls the House of Representatives. (Business Insider)
- 46% of Americans don't know the political party of their local representative. (Washington Post)

- 77% of American Millennials don't know any of the senators from their state. (Politico)
- 63% of Americans can't name a Supreme Court Justice.
- 33% of Americans can't name the Vice President. (Pew Research)
- 23% of Americans don't know we have a National Debt. (Pew Research)

If you are to help a candidate get elected, or you are trying to get elected, the number one thing to do is to inform voters. Nelson Mandela once stated "Education is the most powerful weapon which you can use to change the world." If you campaigned for a candidate, all you have to do sometimes is explain what may seem like simple facts to them.

If you want to get more involved than simply voting, you can get to know candidates that are running, go to town hall meetings, go to city council meetings, join a campaign, volunteer at campaign headquarters, attend rallies, organize rallies, donate to campaigns, get merchandise from candidates, volunteer at polling places, and if you think you have it in you, run for office. If that seems like a lot, then just vote, but vote as an informed citizen. Read political books, follow the news, and most importantly, know the consequences of electing the candidate you support. If you can't explain what will happen when the candidate gets elected or why you should vote for the candidate, then don't vote for that candidate. Finally, know that your vote matters as much as every other vote, and remember: seek something better.

Index

A

by, 6, 8

C

D

has, 7

have, 6-9

he, 10

held, 10

help, 6

House, 6, 8

how, 6-7

however, 7

Hubbard, 10

I

If, 6-8

if, 7

important, 6

improve, 6

In, 6

J

K

never, 8, 10

new, 7-8

next, 8

No, 8

no, 9

Nobody, 8

Nomination, 4

not, 7

O

obtain, 7

occur, 7

Of, 6, 10

of, 6-10

off, 10

on, 6-8, 10

written, 10

Y

years, 10

yet, 7

You, 7

you, 6-7

your, 10

yourself, 6

www.ingramcontent.com/pod-product-compliance
Lightning Source LLC
Chambersburg PA
CBHW030420290526
45786CB00001B/64